Simplify
Your Holiday Season

Turn Seasonal Stress into Holiday Success!

MARCIA RAMSLAND

The Organizing Pro

Previously published in part as *Simplify Your Holidays* by Thomas Nelson (2008) Nashville, TN. Thomas Nelson is a registered trademark of Thomas Nelson, Inc.

The author is represented by the literary agency of Alive Communications, Inc., 7680 Goddard Street, Suite 200, Colorado Springs, Colorado 80920, **www.alivecommunications.com**. Multiple copies or special printing arrangements may be obtained by sending a request through **www.OrganizingPro.com**.

Cover Concept: Maria Keckler, Vineworks Publishing
Cover and Interior Design: Carolyn Gibbs, Viridian Graphics
Author Photo: Nina Jensen, Nina Jensen Studios
Editor: Karen O'Connor, Karen O'Connor Communications
Proofreader: Ruth Ann Dalley

Library of Congress Cataloging-in-Publication Data

Ramsland, Marcia.
Simplify Your Holiday Season: Turn Seasonal Stress into Holiday Success! by Marcia Ramsland.

ISBN 978-1- 6220-9097-6
1. Christmas—United States. 2. Holidays I. Title.

Simplify
Your Holiday Season

❄

Simplifying your holiday season is an opportunity to create positive memories for yourself and those in your life around the three most celebrated holidays at the end of the year — Thanksgiving, Christmas, and New Year's.

Learn how to turn busy holiday stress into seasonal success. This is your year. You can do it!

Simplifying your holiday season is all about . . .

- ✓ Sharing a meaningful Thanksgiving, Christmas, and New Year's with loved ones.

- ✓ Relieving pressure during a typically stressful time of year.

- ✓ Giving gifts from your heart and within your budget.

- ✓ Decorating with just the things you like.

- ✓ Sending cards because you want to, not because you have to.

- ✓ Watching people's faces light up as you deliver gifts or help at a charity.

- ✓ Entertaining to bring people together in an easy way.

- ✓ Participating in the season without feeling overcommitted or under prepared.

- ✓ Saving time, energy, and money.

- ✓ Deciding when enough is enough and stopping to enjoy the season.

- ✓ Finding successful and simple systems that work for you and your lifestyle.

*With a little extra planning, the holiday season can become a time
to look forward to — a time with family and friends, beautiful decorations,
homemade cooking, special events and giving from your heart.*

Books by Marcia Ramsland:

- *Simplify Your Life: Get Organized and Stay That Way!*
- *Simplify Your Time: Stop Running and Start Living!*
- *Simplify Your Space: Create Order and Reduce Stress!*
- *Ages and Stages of Getting Children Organized (Booklet)*
- *Simplify Your Holiday Season: Turn Seasonal Stress into Holiday Success!*
- *Simply December Devotions: 25 Days to Celebrate the Real Meaning of Christmas*

All books available with Free Tips and a DVD Series
"7 Weeks to a NEW Organized You!" at
www.OrganizingPro.com

Welcome!

Dear Friend,

Simplify Your Holiday Season is your opportunity to learn the secret of turning the usual seasonal stress into holiday success. You will learn an easy planning system no matter what day you start your holiday preparations. You will emerge knowing exactly what to do and when to do it.

The three major sections of the book are based on what you experience through the holiday season including: Things to Do, Places to Go, People to See. Read chapters as the season unfolds or review the whole book from beginning to end to take in the big picture.

Dynamic Features beyond the Book

Simplify Your Holiday Season is an annual resource you'll refer to every fall for inspiration and practical reminders. This book entitles you to renewable, bonus features to help you simplify every year, including:

- **The Front Book Pocket.** This is the perfect place to keep annual downloadable forms to keep you on track: The Current Year Holiday Season Calendar Plan, Your Personal Plan, and the Master Gift List form. These forms will keep you on schedule with dates and holiday prep activities to customize your own timeline.
- **Bonus Holiday Charts.** Online at **www.OrganizingPro.com** and at the back of the book are charts covering everything from menus, decorations, address lists, and year-end charitable donations for your personal notes and ideas. Save these to simplify next year even more!
- **Support Group Discussion Questions.** You can get a "Holiday Support Group" or Holiday Partner and go through the season together. Read the chapters, discuss the questions and support one another through the season.
- **Expert 10 Tips.** Every chapter features an expert with their 10 best tips for that topic. You will get to read their succinct tips and hear them personally in the holiday classes to learn even more from their expertise.
- **Online November and December Classes.** New online classes and webinars are offered annually at **www.OrganizingPro.com** that will inspire you for the current year with updates, new classes, support groups, and expert interviews.

The most important key to a calm season is... YOU! That's right. Once you feel in control, you can be the calm person you always dreamed of being, making the whole season enjoyable. My goal is to equip you with practical tools, new ideas, and a sense of anticipation. We can do that, and we will... together. Let's get started!

Warmly,
Marcia Ramsland
—The Organizing Pro and Holiday Coach

Contents

❄

A Word from the Author

I love holiday gatherings with family and friends. One stands out in particular. My friends Ken and Mary were hosting our neighborhood Christmas Party. Everyone was excited. As the party date approached Ken was busy adding holiday decorations outside to greet the party goers. As darkness descended on the night of the party, the house lit up in the most spectacular display from the rooftop eves and windows, right down to moving lighted reindeer on the front lawn.

But as instantly as the light parade began, it suddenly went out! Ken quickly replaced the blown fuse and the light reappeared for about a minute — until it shut down again. The cycle repeated itself so many times we finally all went inside and started the party.

By the end of the evening, people were asking, "Where's Ken?" As we left we thanked poor Ken still on the roof for the great party he had missed. My electrical engineer husband, who had been helping Ken, explained what happened and it sounded like a holiday tip. "The seven light strings were strung end to end and the high current raced through them all only to overload the outlets and blow a fuse. The solution is to connect each light to the source or only string three light sets together."

I smiled as I realized that's exactly what our problem is with the holidays. We function normally all year with "three strings of lights" in our usual lifestyle. Then the holidays arrive with four extra light sets to plug into our calendar — gift shopping, greeting cards, Christmas decorations, and double the number of social events. No wonder the holidays are stressful!

My question to you is, Are you strung too thin at the holidays? There are many reasons the season feels pressure-packed. But let's set a goal to simplify each part and make it easier overall. Once you read this book, you'll know how to overcome seasonal overload.

In this book you will find new ways to look at the season and turn seasonal stress into one of peace. If you are frazzled you will find immediate success this year. If you are ultra-organized, you will have flexible time to help others. Promise me you won't get "strung out" anymore, ok? Let's begin to simplify the season!

Warmly,
Marcia Ramsland
—The Organizing Pro and Holiday Coach

Simplify Your Holiday Season

SECTION 1
Things to Do

❄

1. Get Started Right with 'The Holiday Plan'

2. Gift-Giving Master List and Ideas

3. Holiday Greetings — Your Style, Your Way

4. Holiday Decorations Up and Down Easily

*Nothing is too hard in itself for the holidays. It's all the little things
that add up to cause us stress. Spread them out to remain calm through the season.
Your friends will wonder what you've been up to!*

1

Get Started Right

Simplify the Season with
"A Holiday Season Calendar Plan"

Once you learn the secrets to manage the season successfully,
you'll look forward to the best time of the year,
every year instead of getting caught up in the busyness of the season.

lanning is powerful! And with a good plan and your eye on your calendar, you can simplify your holiday season each year. Instead of playing "catch-up" and feeling stressed, you will experience freedom and calm with the practical Holiday Season Calendar Plan. My motto as a seasoned Professional Organizer is:

If you do anything more than once in life,
organize it and simplify it. That's especially true for the holidays
that come year after year like clockwork.

This means looking for ways to improve anything that you're sure you'll be doing again. When that happens, you'll feel more confident the next time you approach the situation and better results are assured. Let me begin by sharing three tips you can immediately apply to overcome the usual seasonal stress.

A Dramatic Beginning

For many years I had no plan and was overwhelmed by the whole season. It put knots in my stomach and kept me awake at night. I was often stuck in the mall shopping for gifts at the last minute, standing in the rain looking for a "real" Christmas tree late in December, and staying up Christmas Eve wrapping presents... until I figured out a workable plan to manage all the pieces of the holiday puzzle.

With that level of frustration I actually sat down at the kitchen table after Christmas one day determined to get control of the season. I spread out calendars and gift lists from the past several years. My goal was to figure out why I was always feeling behind and change that. That year I had told myself to start early. I did shop earlier, but I had forgotten to wrap the presents. I was up wrapping on Christmas Eve — again. It was time to discover the solution to an annual stressful problem. And I did.

Discovery #1 — Pick the Best Start Date

As I compared the calendars from past years, it suddenly dawned on me—there was a pattern the way I was managing it all. I had been counting on getting through Thanksgiving before I started. And Thanksgiving was a floating holiday on a different date every year. That was my problem! Sometimes Thanksgiving was four and a half weeks before Christmas, and sometimes it was only three and a half weeks. That's why people say, "Christmas came early this year." Sometimes it does.

I realized many people, myself included, have used Thanksgiving to trigger serious action steps for the December holidays. It didn't seem right to skip over Thanksgiving to get a jump-start on Christmas. On the other hand, if I waited to shop for Christmas until after Thanksgiving I'd be caught in the middle of a mall with throngs of shoppers.

The solution came clear when I noticed one particular holiday occurs exactly eight weeks before Christmas.  Halloween is always on October 31 and is important to note because the next day— November 1 - you can kick off your holiday plan every year! I just created a plan by inputting all the holiday activities into those eight weeks. Suddenly the holidays were manageable when the plan was redesigned.

The key date—November 1—means you have eight weeks until December 25 to easily navigate the season. Even if you don't begin on November 1, you have a calendar structure whenever you do begin. I have included an 8-Week, 4-Week Plan, 2-Week Plan and a 10-Day Countdown so you can be on track and calm whatever day you start.

Discovery #2 — Prepare for Stress in the Last Three Weeks

My second turning point came when I noticed on past calendars that the majority of holiday events landed in the three weeks right before Christmas. Children's school parties, the neighborhood cookie exchange, civic symphony concerts, church events, friends' Open Houses and an office luncheon the last day before vacation.

No wonder we get frazzled buying gifts and participating in the busiest social season of the year. All these things are good, but it's plain stressful to be listening to the Hallelujah Chorus thinking about how many things you can pick up on the way home and still purchase online gifts with "expedite shipping" costs to save the day.

What's the solution? Start all the gift shopping and card sending BEFORE you decorate and the holiday events begin. It is the easiest way to stay sane and not be frustrated with the whole process. (But we also have lots of tips if you're a bit behind this year or dealing with an unexpected crisis.)

Discovery #3 — Simplify Decorations Early

My third discovery came when I was taking down my holiday decorations. I noticed some I'd never put up, and decided it was just too much work to deal with all of them each year. So I carefully selected items, keeping some and putting aside others to donate.

But alas, when I arrived at the charity, the man laughed and said, "We don't have room to store old decorations until next year any more than you do. Donate them right after Thanksgiving." That was a reality check. I was giving up valuable space at home to store these for eleven months of the year and complaining when I had to put them up (but always glad once they were). What's the answer? Don't wait for the weather to put you in the right mood. Just pick a date or weekend to put your decorations up and enjoy them the whole season. It will help you "feel" festive sooner.

Start the Season with "The Holiday Season Calendar Plan!"

Once you know you can organize your holidays whether you have eight weeks, four weeks or one week left before Christmas, it's time to begin. Plan on paper, work your plan, and adjust when things get off course. It's easier to get a little done each day, rather than under the pressure of the last minute. You save time and money while enjoying peace of mind with a plan in place.

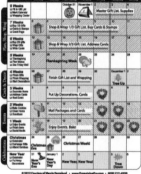

The 2012 Holiday Season 8-Week Calendar Plan

If you improve something each year, you will find the holidays are more of a joy and less of a chore as time goes by. This year choose the Holiday Season Calendar Plan based on today's date whether you are eight weeks, four weeks, or two weeks away from Christmas.

Picture yourself sitting down with a cup of coffee, enjoying a calm evening at home with your holiday decorations around you. Holiday music is softly playing and you have time to relax, read a magazine, play a game with your kids, or call a friend. This scenario is one of the many results of simplifying the holiday season.

> *To simplify the holiday season is to transform something complicated into something easy. The holiday season from Thanksgiving, Christmas, and New Year's qualifies as the busiest and most complicated time of the year — until you know the secrets to simplify it.*

Each year I hear women say, "This system works! When is your new Holiday Season Calendar Plan coming out? I love how it shows me if I'm on track." And at the end of the season, women have sailed through the holidays and actually enjoyed them.

But not just women. A couple wives reported their husbands said, "What weekend do we put up the decorations?" And *they* took on the task! Everyone likes to know what's coming and the best benefit is that others contribute to make the season festive and memorable! Let me share with you all my secrets to make it a success.

Simplify Your Holiday Season
with SOS Pyramid

To simplify anything in life follow these three steps in the SOS Pyramid I unveiled in my book, *Simplify Your Space.* For the holiday time pressures, it works the same way.

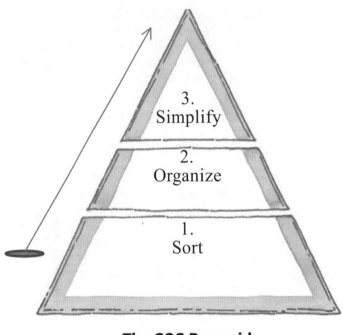

The SOS Pyramid

Aspire to move up the pyramid each year and the holidays will get easier!

Step 1: Sort Your Tasks and Assign Dates. Update your activities on one calendar, fill in your Master Gift List, plan a decorating weekend, and Christmas card list onto the holiday charts so you can see how complicated or reasonable your holidays actually are.

Step 2: Organize the Steps in Each Task. Arrange your calendar to balance the pressures of your current life by planning early how everything will fit. You can only do so much in a day or weekend so include just what is meaningful to you this season. Four nights away from home per week is the max we recommend to keep from stressing.

Step 3: Simplify Activities by Picking Your Priorities. Focus on what's meaningful by leaving out draining tasks and investing in those you enjoy. Fewer quality activities and tasks may be just what you need to keep your season on a manageable level.

Now You Are Ready! Let's Begin

The Holiday Plan is the view of the calendar and holiday activities planned out for you in order to sail smoothly through the season. It is a combination of both. It includes a time sequence to allow you to get things done without.

What is the Holiday Calendar Plan in a Nutshell?

Phase 1: Plan, Shop, Wrap
Phase 2: Decorate and Mail
Phase 3: Celebrations • Christmas Week • New Year's Week

These are laid out on our Holiday Season Calendar Plan as a sample to follow. You can personalize it on Your Calendar Plan at **www.OrganizingPro.com** which has the dates for this year already printed. You can also customize it on your own monthly calendar.

Why Do I Need a New Holiday Calendar Each Year?

The calendar dates change every year for the major holidays. This can mess up your plan from one year to the next. We do promise to provide updated Holiday Calendar Plans that you can download yearly at **http://www.OrganizingPro.com.**

Which Holiday Season Calendar Plan Do I Use: 8-Week, 4-Week, or 2-Week?

That's easy. Find out what today's date is and pick the calendar that includes the date you plan to begin your preparations. That's the Holiday Season Calendar Plan you can post or put in the front pocket of this book.

How Can I Follow the Plan?

It's not hard. Just keep the current year plan in the front pocket of this book, on your refrigerator, bathroom mirror, or by your computer. If you get off track, rearrange your activities. If you see you can't do it all, simply cut back or ask for help.

How Do I Get Support to Keep Going?

The best way is to either join our Online Classes in November and December, get a group of friends to form a Holiday Support Group (either in person or by phone), or get a Holiday Buddy and check in with each other every week through the season.

What Do I Do First?

Download the actual Holiday Season Calendar Plan for this year from **www.OrganizingPro.com** and place it either in the front pocket of your book or post it where you will see it. Highlight calendar dates that you will have work or school vacations or guests.

Not Ready to Do That?

That's fine. Simply read the rest of the book and come back to download the Holiday Season Plan when you need it. The first step to simplifying anything is to plan it on your calendar.

The Holiday Season
8-Week Calendar Plan Checklist

Check off the items as you do them. Assign the tasks to days on your calendar.

8 Weeks Before
- ☐ Fill in this year's Gift List with names and gift ideas following last year's Gift List.
- ☐ Mark your personal calendar in an 8-week countdown like the sample page.
- ☐ Organize your Gift-Wrapping Center supplies. List what you need.

7 Weeks Before
- ☐ Shop for and wrap one-third of your gifts list.
- ☐ Gather Christmas cards, return address labels, and stamps.
- ☐ Start an Event Worksheet for any holiday event you are hosting.

6 Weeks Before
- ☐ Shop for and wrap an additional one-third of your gift list.
- ☐ Update your address list and write Christmas cards.
- ☐ Shop November sale days for bargains for people on your Gift list.

5 Weeks Before *(Change steps with Week 4 depending when Thanksgiving is.)*
- ☐ Focus on Thanksgiving preparations. Take a family photo for Christmas card.
- ☐ Plan the Bonus Thanksgiving Weekend—shop, decorate, or relax.
- ☐ Use the weekend to move toward Christmas preparations.

4 Weeks Before *(Change steps with Week 5 depending when Thanksgiving is.)*
- ☐ Shop for and wrap the final one-third of your total gifts.
- ☐ Purchase special baking ingredients you will need, such as nuts, almond paste, etc.
- ☐ Gather Thanksgiving centerpiece, menu, table settings, napkins, and place cards.

3 Weeks Before
- ☐ Sign and mail Christmas cards and holiday packages.
- ☐ Decorate your Christmas tree and home for the holidays.
- ☐ Begin reading your inspirational Christmas books and magazines.

2 Weeks Before
- ☐ Bake cookies and clean house.
- ☐ Join in a Christmas event for neighbors, coworkers, or charity.
- ☐ Deliver charity gifts and mail year-end contributions.

1 Week Before
- ☐ Bake your favorite traditional cookies and foods.
- ☐ Donate time to charities that need extra help.
- ☐ Deliver gifts to coworkers, neighbors, school, or others.

Celebrate Christmas ("The" Week)
- ☐ Celebrate with the gifts, food, and people you planned.
- ☐ Spend time reflecting on the meaning of Christmas and/or attend a service.
- ☐ Take pictures to capture the memories and place them in a holiday photo book.

New Year's Week- Bonus Week to Clean Up—New Year, New You!
- ☐ Write thank-you notes, and put away holiday decorations soon.
- ☐ Get your home, family, and office in order for the New Year.
- ☐ Fill in your journal *"The Best Things That Happened This Holiday Season."*

The Holiday Season
8-Week Calendar Plan

		Monday	Tuesday	Wednesday	Thursday	Friday	Saturday	Sunday
Plan, Shop, Wrap	**8 Weeks** ❑ Fill in Gift List ❑ Mark Calendar ❑ Wrapping Center			October 31	November 1	2 Master Gift List. Supplies	3	4
	7 Weeks ❑ Buy 1/3 Gifts ❑ Cards & Stamps ❑ Event Page	5	6 Shop & Wrap 1/3 Gift List. Buy Cards & Stamps	7	8	9	10	11
	6 Weeks ❑ Buy 2/3 gifts ❑ Wrap Gifts ❑ Write Cards	12	13 Shop & Wrap 2/3 Gift List. Address Cards	14	15	16	17	18
	5 Weeks ❑ Thanksgiving ❑ Plan Menus ❑ Use Friday Well	19	20 **Thanksgiving Week**	21	22	23	24	25
Cards & Decor	**4 Weeks** ❑ Finish Gifts ❑ Finish Wrapping ❑ Start Decorations	26	27 Finish Gift List and Wrapping	28	29	30	December 1 **Tree Up**	2
	3 Weeks ❑ Decorate Home ❑ Address Cards ❑ Host Event	3	4 Put Up Decorations. Cards	5	6	7	8	9
Events	**2 Weeks** ❑ Bake Cookies ❑ Clean Home ❑ Donations	10	11 Mail Packages and Cards	12	13	14	15	16
	1 Week ❑ Enjoy Events ❑ Finish Bake ❑ Social Media	17	18 Enjoy Events. Bake	19	20	21	22	23
Celebrations	**Christmas** ❑ Celebrate! ❑ Exchange Gifts ❑ Attend Services	24 **Christmas Eve**	25 **Christmas Day**	26 **Christmas Week!**	27	28	29	30
	New Year ❑ Celebrate! ❑ Put Away Decorations	31 **New Year's Eve**	January 1 **New Year's Day**	2 **New Year, New You!**	3	4	5 **Tree Down**	6

© 2012 Courtesy of Marcia Ramsland • www.OrganizingPro.com • (858) 217–6320

The Holiday Season
4-Week Calendar Plan Checklist

Check off the items as you do them. Fill in the blank 4-Week Plan with dates, and assign the tasks to specific days. More explanation for each task is found in the related section.

4 Weeks Before

☐ Review last year's Gift List. Then fill in this year's Gift List with names and any gift ideas.

☐ Stock your Gift-Wrapping Center with supplies, such as wrapping paper, bows, tags, gift boxes, and the like.

☐ Update your address list and write Christmas cards.

3 Weeks Before

☐ Sign, seal, and mail Christmas cards and holiday packages.

☐ Decorate your Christmas tree and home for the holidays.

☐ Shop for and wrap the first half of your total gifts.

☐ Begin reading your inspirational Christmas books and magazines.

2 Weeks Before

☐ Shop for and wrap the last half of your total gifts.

☐ Attend Christmas events for neighbors, coworkers, or charity.

☐ Mail year-end contributions.

1 Week Before

☐ Donate time to charities that need extra help.

☐ Deliver gifts to coworkers, neighbors, school, and others.

☐ Bake favorite cookies and clean house.

"The Holiday Season Calendar Plan" *is your guide to turn the most stressful time of the year into seasonal success year after year. It is your answer to finding peace and calm when life is already busy and complicated in December. It's a way to fine tune on paper the many items you lay awake worrying about and trying to remember to do.*

The Holiday Season
4-Week Calendar Plan

	Monday	Tuesday	Wednesday	Thursday	Friday	Saturday	Sunday
4 Weeks ❑ Fill in Gift List ❑ Stock Gift-Wrapping Center ❑ Start December 1–25 Reading				Nov 29	30	Dec 1	2
					Shop & Wrap 1/2 List		
3 Weeks ❑ Christmas Cards ❑ Mail Cards & Packages ❑ Tree Up & Decorate Inside	3	4	5	6	7	8 Tree Up	9
	Write Cards & Mail Packages				Decorate		
2 Weeks ❑ Bake Cookies ❑ Clean 1/2 Home ❑ Host Own Event	10	11	12	13	14	15	16
	Shop & Wrap 1/2 Gift List. Mail. Donations						
1 Week ❑ Enjoy Events ❑ Deliver Gifts ❑ Clean Other 1/2 Home	17	18	19	20	21	22	23
	Baking Week		Deliver Gifts			Charity Time	
Christmas ❑ Celebrate! ❑ Exchange Gifts ❑ Attend Services	24	25	26	27	28	29	30
		Celebrate			Relax and Send Thank You's		
New Year ❑ Finish Notebook Pages ❑ Put Away Decorations ❑ Cleanup for New Year	31	Jan 1	2	3	4	5 Tree Down	6
	Get Home & Office in Order. New Year, New You! Put Decorations Away						

Side tabs: Plan, Shop, Wrap | Mail & Decor | Celebrations

The Holiday Season
2-Week Calendar Plan Checklist

Check off the items as you do them. Fill in the blank 2-Week Plan with dates, and assign the tasks to specific days. More explanation for each task is found in the related section.

2 Weeks Before

☐ Shop for and wrap the first half of the gifts on your list.

☐ Attend holiday events for neighbors, coworkers, or charity.

☐ Decorate your Christmas tree and home for the holidays.

1 Week Before

☐ Shop for and wrap the last half of the gifts on your list.

☐ Bake a few favorite cookies and clean house.

☐ Donate time to charities that need extra help.

Celebrate Christmas ("The" Week)

☐ Celebrate with the gifts, food, and people you planned.

☐ Spend time reflecting on the real meaning of Christmas and/or attending a Christmas service.

☐ Take pictures to capture the memories and store in your holiday photo file.

Clean Up—New Year, New You! (Bonus Week)

☐ Clean up, write thank-you notes, and put away decorations.

☐ Fill in your journal page "The Best Things That Happened This Christmas."

☐ Get your home and office in order for the New Year.

> *With the 8-Week, 4-Week, 2-Week or 10-Day Countdown Plan, you can stay ahead of the game and sail through the season. Whichever plan you choose, check it often to stay on track and minimize seasonal stress.*

The Holiday Season
2-Week Calendar Plan

	Monday	Tuesday	Wednesday	Thursday	Friday	Saturday	Sunday
2 Weeks ☐ Buy 1/2 gifts ☐ Enjoy Events ☐ Decorate Home	10	11	12	13	14	15	16
	Shop & Wrap 1/2 Gift List. Mail. Donations						
1 Week ☐ Finish Gifts ☐ Bake Cookies ☐ Clean Home	17	18	19	20	21	22	23
	Baking Week		Deliver Gifts			Charity Time	
Christmas ☐ Celebrate! ☐ Exchange Gifts ☐ Attend Services	24	25	26	27	28	29	30
	Celebrate				Relax and Send Thank You's		
New Year ☐ Finish Notebook Pages ☐ Put Away Decorations ☐ Cleanup for New Year	31	Jan 1	2	3	4	5 **Tree Down**	6
	Get Home & Office in Order. New Year, New You! Put Decorations Away						

Mail & Decor

Celebrations

© **2012 Courtesy of Marcia Ramsland** • **www.OrganizingPro.com** • **(858) 217–6320**

The 10-Day Countdown Plan

It's not too late! You can still pull together a successful Christmas in a few days! (Check off the items as you do them. Fill in the blank 10-Day Countdown Plan with dates, and assign the tasks to specific days. More explanation for each task is found in the related section.)

○ **10 Days**—Make your final gift list on the Master Gift List.

○ **9 Days**—Finish shopping at one store or one online store.

○ **8 Days**—Wrap remaining gifts and send out final Christmas cards.

○ **7 Days**—Put up remaining decorations and enjoy a holiday movie.

○ **6 Days**—Bake a favorite Christmas cookie or nutbread recipe.

○ **5 Days**—Vacuum and give a quick cleaning to your home.

○ **4 Days**—Plan your meals and bring in final groceries.

○ **3 Days**—Confirm Christmas Day plans with others.

○ **2 Days**—Read and reflect on the real meaning of Christmas and attend services.

○ **1 Day**—Celebrate with Christmas gifts, family, and a time of thankfulness.

Comments from Holiday Class Participants

"I learned that the three weeks before Christmas are too busy. Start now!"
— Colleen P.

"The first thing I'm going to simplify my holidays is get a calendar and write events and plan gift gifting."
— Miriam W.

"I appreciated your helpfulness in getting more organized and simplifying things in order to enjoy the holidays."
— Patricia V.

"I decided to "enjoy" the holidays instead of just surviving."
— Linda S.

10 Relationship Tips for the Holidays
BY PAM FARREL, AUTHOR, SPEAKER, AND RELATIONSHIP EXPERT

While simplifying your holiday season, take time for relationships to thrive, not just survive. People are more important than things, especially at this time of year. Here are some principles to apply to your relationships during this festive season.

1 **Center Your Heart.** Focus on the true, deeper meaning of the holiday celebrations of Thanksgiving, Christmas, and New Year's. This will help everyone become easier to get along with because the heart of the holiday will remain intact.

2 **Hear What Your Friends and Family are Voicing as Their Stress.** Listen carefully to those around you — a gift that will lower their stress.

3 **Reach Out as a Family to Help Others.** Keep the proper perspective of what is really important in life by looking for ways to help others. Everyone has something to give.

4 **Invest in Memories, not Material Goods.** Make time for family baking, tree decorating, or board games..

5 **Speak Your Love in Words.** The best gift you can give another person is personal words of praise, gratitude, and acknowledgment from your lips.

6 **Take Time for Relationships.** The greatest gift you can give your spouse, children, and friends is harmony at home.

7 **Take Time to Reach Out to Extended Family.** Visit or call grandparents, aunts, and uncles. If possible, use modern technology like Skype to connect.

8 **Assume Nothing.** Ask those who are celebrating with you what their expectations are, and communicate the plan clearly so people feel informed..

9 **Stay Flexible.** Don't be a Christmas Scrooge ordering family around. Instead slow the pace, gather consensus, and give options to create an environment of connecting and sharing.

10 **Express Your Joy.** Make memories by making the most of all your relationships!

Pam Farrel is a relationship specialist, international speaker, and author of more than twenty-five books, including best-selling Men Are like Waffles, Women Are like Spaghetti, The Marriage Code, The 10 Best Decisions a Single Can Make. *The Farrels' books have sold more than a half million copies. They are frequent guests on radio and TV. Visit* **love-wise.com**

Start Right with a Holiday Plan

1. Choose a main calendar (either ours or your monthly calendar) that you'll use as your main planning calendar and keep it in one location. Mark holiday events, vacations, and holiday prep activities on it. This is the key to simplifying the season.
2. Number the weeks in the margin of your monthly calendar like a countdown to Christmas week — 3, 2, 1, 0 (or should we say "Celebrate!")
3. Refer to the Holiday Season Calendar Plan as you do the rest of the chapters in this book. Follow the overview of the season while learning ways to organize and simplify the details.

Personal Reflection

1. The holidays are best when I _____

   _____

2. What I like about the holiday season is _____

   _____

3. One thing I'd like to change about my holiday season _____

   _____

Holiday Support Group Discussion Questions

1. What's a favorite holiday memory you've had in recent years?

2. Share what you usually do for putting up holiday decorations for Christmas.

3. What do you usually do for Thanksgiving?

4. Who enjoys the holidays the most in your family?

5. When do you tend to start getting ready for the holidays?

6. If you could change one thing this year about the holidays, what would it be?

7. Something I'd really like to simplify about the holidays is _____

   _____

> *Remember it's not the things we do that make us tired. It's the things left undone that wear us out!*

2

Gift Giving Success

Important Gift-Giving Strategies

A gift given is a double joy for two people: the receiver lights up with being remembered, and you, the giver, are rewarded for a kindness shared.

Gift giving can be one of the biggest stresses of the holidays, beginning with deciding what to buy, where to buy it, followed by time spent wrapping and delivering it. Not anymore! Once you have a gift list full of ideas, past lists for reference, and gift-wrapping supplies on hand, holiday shopping can begin to take shape. A pretty wrapping paper, sparkly bow, and signed card are our goal—and done long before Christmas Eve.

No more back-of-the-envelope planning as you head out to the mall. Keep your list on hand and simplify the abundance of choices by sticking to one or two stores or online businesses.

Organize Your Master Gift List

Begin by filling in the Gift Giving form, listing people to whom you plan to give a gift, ideas of what to get them, and a budget amount. (Yes, it's wise to think about money beforehand and shop creatively to stick to it). Use the same form from year to year, and you'll spend less time worrying about whether you remembered everyone. You'll find the more organized your records from last year are, the less trouble you will have thinking of new ideas this year.

Who do we put on the list? Start with the most important and closest family members: spouse, children, parents, siblings. Then add others as you have the time or energy. Use as many lines as you need for each person.

How many people can you handle buying gifts for each year? Somewhere between six to ten people may be comfortable for some of us. Others in the midst of raising children may give to immediate and extended family totaling twenty to thirty people. When your list of names is manageable, you will enjoy the season more. Stop whatever is frustrating!

> *Gift giving is an inside-out feeling wrapped in a box.*

For everyone there comes a time when you need to simplify and not feel guilty about doing it. For example, agree with your family that when your nieces and nephews graduate from high school (or turn sixteen years old), you stop buying gifts for him or her. Or when the extended family gathering becomes too large, you might start drawing names so each person brings a nice gift for only one other person. Or you might move to giving birthday gifts to minimize the holiday gift giving overload.

The important thing is to learn your limits, and writing the list on paper gives you the perfect overview. Fine-tune it each year until you are comfortable with it.

Who Should I Put On My Gift List?

The rule of thumb is to include closest family and those with whom you have a history of exchanging gifts. Don't make it complicated by adding more people. Often a Christmas card greeting is all that's needed. Above all, limit your list to a comfortable number of people.

Here is a list of memory jogger names. Put a check mark beside those you include in your gift list; put an X by those you do not.

✔	X		✔	X	
		Husband			**Father-in-law**
		Wife			**Sister-in-law(s)**
		Daughter(s)			**Brother-in-law(s)**
		Son(s)			**Roommate(s)**
		Mother			**Boss(es)**
		Father			**Secretary**
		Grandmother(s)			**Coworkers**
		Grandfather(s)			**Teacher(s)**
		Grandchildren			**Baby Sitter**
		Sister(s)			**Neighbors**
		Brother(s)			**Friends**
		Mother-in-law			**Others**

List the names in the same order each year so you can easily refer to what you did last year. That way you don't have to wonder, *What did I give them already?* Now you'll know!

Look for a gift with a surprise element. That means it is not expected and is a surprise in some way, but also something the receiver really likes or is passionately interested in. That's how you create the "magic" of gift-giving at Christmas.

Simplify with a Gift Theme

Simplify your gift shopping by visiting only certain types of stores for everyone on your list. Choose a giving "theme" for the year, but get a different gift in that theme for each person so it is personalized. For example, all the women get jewelry, spa baskets, gift certificates, or robes. Men get sporting event tickets, restaurant certificates, or tools. Sweaters, CDs, DVDs, or books all make great themes too.

A Dozen Gift Theme Ideas

1. Sweaters for everyone
2. Favorite restaurant or movie gift cards
3. Gloves and mittens
4. DVDs
5. CDs or books
6. Tickets to a play, musical, or retreat
7. Photo book or digital camera
8. A trip or the latest technology
9. Favorite magazine plus a year's subscription
10. Chocolate, nuts, or gourmet food basket
11. Spa, massage, or bath items
12. Jewelry, purse, or accessories

For Men
(Practical is generally better than sentimental.)

Tool kit
Computer software
Travel clock
TV, radio, cell phone
Favorite hobby gear
Sporting event tickets
Camping equipment
Hunting or fishing gear

For Kids
(It's best to ask for a prioritized list!)

Age-appropriate toys
Clothes
Hobby or sports gear
Book, CD, or DVD
Adventure pass or certificate
Computer games
Movie tickets

For Women
(Personal is generally better than practical.)

Spa basket or gift certificate
Clothes
Candles
Cookbook
Chocolate anything
Jewelry

General

Calendar
Desk clock
Paperweight
Food basket
Chocolate or other candy
Book or audio book

Important Gift-Giving Strategies

*G*ift giving can either simplify or complicate your life. Keep it simple as you shop and make your plans. Take notes and you will get better each year. The sooner you get started the less stress you will encounter and the more likely you are to get a gift that is sure to make the receiver smile.

1. **The Mall or Specialty Stores.** Shop where you get the best results. Keep track of where you buy most of your gifts from year to year and head there first. They will have new merchandise each year that will probably work well for you again.

2. **Shopping Online.** Order your gifts online and use the "Ship Direct" option to send the gift to someone else in their household to wrap and hide for you. Offer to return the favor. Also keep a list of online shopping items, including expected arrival dates, order confirmation numbers, and shipping costs. Going online may allow you to have it bought and shipped in less time and money than physically going out to the store would do.

3. **Gifts to Mail.** Order your gifts online and use the "Ship Direct" option to send them directly to the intended recipients. Be sure to purchase and ship gifts by the first week of December to ensure their arriving on time.

4. **Practical vs. Sentimental Gifts.** Buy practical gifts for practical people and sentimental gifts for sentimental people. This makes your gift more likely to hit the mark. For clues about which is which, note what they give you. For instance, if you usually get kitchen gadgets from your mother, that tells you she likes practical gifts.

5. **Children's Gifts.** Shop for children first as their gift choices can run out of stock. Keep one gift slot for each child open until it's nearly Christmas, because they often think of something new they want based on holiday advertisements. They will probably be the most delighted with their gifts, so try to think about what a child would most like to open.

6. **Handmade Gifts.** Make a schedule by mapping out on your calendar how much you can realistically accomplish each week before Christmas—whether it's a large project or a few small ornaments. Then schedule crafting times as appointments and stick to them. Major projects, such as a full-size quilt, should be started earlier in the year and, hopefully, completed by Halloween so you can avoid the stress of trying to complete them during the holiday rush.

Remember, a gift shows you had the person in your thoughts, and a note on your card tells them why you thought they'd like it. Gift giving is a skill to learn.

Master Gift List

_____ (year)

Done X	#	Person	Gift Ideas	$ Budget	Actual Gift and from Where	$ Cost
	*					
	1					
	2					
	3					
	4					
	5					
	6					
	7					
	8					
	9					
	10					
	11					
	12					
			Total	$		$

The Master Gift List will save you time and money. Available at **http://www.OrganizingPro.com**

Supplies On Hand

Year_____

◯ Wrapping paper (___ rolls ___ squares)	Ways I Simplified Wrapping...
◯ Bows (_____ ribbons)	
◯ Tissue paper (_____ sheets)	
◯ Gift tags (_____ tags)	
◯ Scotch tape	Supplies I Need for Next Year...
◯ Scissors	
◯ A working pen	

Year_____

◯ Wrapping paper (___ rolls ___ squares)	Ways I Simplified Wrapping...
◯ Bows (_____ ribbons)	
◯ Tissue paper (_____ sheets)	
◯ Gift tags (_____ tags)	
◯ Scotch tape	Supplies I Need for Next Year...
◯ Scissors	
◯ A working pen	

Year_____

◯ Wrapping paper (___ rolls ___ squares)	Ways I Simplified Wrapping...
◯ Bows (_____ ribbons)	
◯ Tissue paper (_____ sheets)	
◯ Gift tags (_____ tags)	
◯ Scotch tape	Supplies I Need for Next Year...
◯ Scissors	
◯ A working pen	

A Gift-Wrapping Center

Create a gift-wrapping center to solve many of those late night wrapping dilemmas. Stock one wrapping box with supplies to store under your bed, in a hall closet, or an easily accessible place. Simplify your holiday wrapping by using all rolls of paper, or all folded squares of paper to keep your wrapping center tidy. Buy a two- or three-color scheme of paper, perhaps using large print, small print, and solid-colored wrapping paper. Warehouse clubs and discount stores often sell wrapping paper bundled in coordinating colors and styles or large rolls of reversible paper.

Also bring home fresh tissue paper to perk up any reused box or gift bag, and remember to ask for a box when you purchase gifts. These are often free and will reduce your expenses.

Stock Your Gift-Wrapping Center

- Various size gift boxes and bags
- Wrapping paper
  (same size rolls or squares)
- Bows and ribbons
- Tissue paper
- Gift tags
- Scotch tape
- Scissors
- A working pen

Complete your package wrapping with a bow for packages you deliver in person, and ribbons for packages that must be mailed. Don't forget to purchase or make matching gift tags with room to write a sentence of warmth and love for the recipient. People often save the tags longer than the gifts!

To: Mom,
Here's a gift for your favorite hobby that you do so well. Love, Lisa

Gift Tag Example:

Always keep a dedicated pen, scissors, and Scotch tape in the Gift-Wrap Center that you don't take to use anywhere else in the house! You don't want to lose time hunting for supplies when you start wrapping.

Once you have purchased a gift, be sure to get it wrapped soon to complete the process. Store the gifts under your Christmas tree, in a closet, or in a hiding place noted on your Master Gift List.

To keep things a further secret, put the number of the gift from your Master Gift List on the gift, and replace it with the actual tag the night before the gifts are opened.

Gifts will be more of a surprise if they are wrapped rather than discovered sitting out. They are easy to wrap if you have your supplies on hand and easily accessible.

Stay Organized with a Holiday Notebook

Keep all your plans, purchase receipts, and celebration ideas in one holiday notebook. A 3-ring notebook with a holiday picture (available at www.organizingpro.com) inserted into the front cover is your tool to stay organized year after year. The tabs can be purchased at an office supply store and listed as below. Keep the Holiday Notebook available in your kitchen or home office.

1 CALENDARS Keep the current year's Holiday Season Calendar Plan in the front. Store your yearly Holiday Plans here so you can refer back to what weeks and weekends you did activities last year.

2 GIFTS Keep your current Master Gift List at the front of this section so you can regularly list ideas and update purchases. Check off with a red pen if is wrapped and where it is stored (downstairs closet, under the stairway or what box in the garage).

3 CARDS Keep your Christmas card address list here, either handwritten on our form or printed from your computer. Include regular mailed card address and email distribution lists. Be sure to put the year at the top of each page so it's easy to update.

4 DECORATIONS Add your list and snapshots of decorations as you placed them in your home. This will be a time-saving reference for next year.

5 RECIPES Food is another major item to consider during the holidays so keep your favorite recipes and menus in this section. It will be easy to get started baking your favorite Christmas cookies and nutbreads ahead of time. Include your holiday menus and make notes about what worked well. Next year will be a breeze.

6 THANKSGIVING This tab with photos, notes, and menu will make next year easier, especially regarding what to do on the days before Thanksgiving Thursday. Include the time to start cooking the turkey and what time you served dinner. Listing specific details helps you simplify.

7 CHRISTMAS Keep your Notes Page here as a memory jogger for next year. Include photos of family opening presents, eating together, and your journal page of "The Best Things that Happened This Christmas" year by year. You'll love the summary.

8 SPECIAL Keep any special pages like Holiday Movie List, Charitable Donation List, Event Steps you planned or Goals for the New Year here. This is your section for those individual summary pages you don't know what to do with.

Keep all your holiday organizing and plans in one place so everything is centralized and not floating around on scraps of paper. Keep your notebook next to your calendar at home or someplace that curious children and family will not find it. This will be your personal resource to use year after year to simplify your life during the holidays.

Think of the possibilities for a calm season if you kept all your holiday ideas in one place, followed the Holiday Season Calendar Plan, and cleaned up your notes for next year. You really could be organized and less stressed for the holidays! Get a Notebook and start today.

10 Money-Saving Holiday Gift Tips
BY ELLIE KAY, AMERICA'S FAMILY FINANCIAL EXPERT™

The average family will create enough credit card debt at Christmas that it will take until the following May to pay it off! There is a less expensive way to survive.

1 **Strategize.** Decide which gifts you want and match them with sale ads. Check off the items on your Master Gift List and note any special limitations (i.e. price only effective for three hours, limit two per person). Prioritize the stores where you'll shop according to limitations and values.

2 **Shop for Comparisons.** Once you locate the make and model of a gift you want to purchase, do a search at Bing.com, Slickdeals.com, or Mysimon.com. When you find the best price, print it out and take it into your local store to see if the manager will match the price.

3 **Save when Shopping Online.** For online coupons, codes for discounts and free shipping, go to RetailMeNot.com, Dealhunting.com or CouponCabin.com.

4 **Split It.** Follow the divide-and-conquer rule by shopping with a friend or your spouse. If there are multiple purchase discounts, such as "buy two and get the second one at half-price" or a two-for-one special, you can go together and split the savings, thus taking advantage of the offer.

5 **Save by Baking.** Early in the season, my kids help me make various sweetbreads to freeze. When it comes time to give gifts to teachers or friends, we tie the breads with raffia, cranberries and voila! These gifts taste great and save money.

6 **Specify.** During the year, set aside a specific "cash" budget each month to use for Christmas. Don't use credit cards unless you know you can pay them at the end of the month.

7 **Stick to Your Guns.** You may be tempted to keep buying even after you've conquered your list. You can go broke saving money, so stick to your budget.

8 **Simplify.** When my hubby and I had five babies in the first seven years of marriage, we came up with the "three-gift rule." We modeled our gift-giving after the three gifts brought to the Christ child. We chose three simple, yet nice presents per child. It still works!

9 **Supervise.** Take younger children to the local Dollar Store for their Christmas shopping for friends and family. Give them an appropriate budget and money, and then let them choose.

10 **Steal It.** Set aside money for after-Christmas sales. You can oftentimes get nonperishable gifts from 50 to 75 percent off retail and save them for next year. That's practically a steal!

Ellie Kay is the best-selling author of fourteen books, including The Little Book of Big Savings *and a frequent guest on ABC, CBS, CNBC, CNN, and Fox News. She has appeared on over 600 radio stations and presents to audiences as large as eight thousand from California to China. She and her husband, Bob, have seven children and live in Palmdale, California. Visit **elliekay.com***

Gift-Giving Success

1. Simplify your gift giving by starting with a Master Gift List. Print out ours or create your own. Keep it in one place that you—and no one else—can access easily. ☺
2. Simplify further with a category theme or the Three-Gift Rule Expert Ellie Kay mentioned in her 10 Money Saving Tips on Holiday Gifts.
3. Organize your Gift Wrap Center and wrap early.

Personal Reflection

1. My gift-giving works best when I _____

_____

2. What I like about giving gifts is _____

_____

3. What I'd like to improve about gift-giving is _____

_____

Group Discussion Questions

1. Have you started shopping for gifts and when did you start?

2. Have you made out a Master Gift List?

3. Do you wrap presents as you get them or wait until you have a lot of them?

4. Who is your most difficult person to shop for?

5. Do you know how much you spend on gifts each year?

6. What is your best (or funniest) memory of someone opening your gift?

7. Something I'd really like to simplify about my gift-giving is _____

_____

> *Wrap and label your gifts within a day or two of purchasing them. Picture yourself waking up rested for Christmas Eve and Christmas Day. Reward yourself when all your gifts are wrapped by going out for lunch with a friend or shopping for something for yourself.*

3

Holiday Greetings

Find Your Style and Keep it Simple

Sending holiday greeting cards is like the Girl Scout motto, "Make new friends, but keep the old. One is silver and the other's gold." Keep in touch with your prized "gold" friends of the past and include your new "silver" friends of more recent days. Life is rich when you have both!

One thing that is sure to make people smile is a Christmas card from you! A holiday greeting builds connection and warmth at the holiday season whether it's sent through the mail, by email, or Social Media. It is also an easy way to keep in touch annually and make up for missed good intentions during the year.

The holidays are a perfect reason to connect with your wider networks of friends, family and clients, but alas it is the busiest time of year to add one more thing. What's the solution? Personalize a system that works for you so you can get it done easily and successfully. Pick a style and organize your address list and you'll actually look forward to it.

Five Popular Styles of Holiday Greetings

Picture yourself with a cup of coffee, holiday music playing, and a clean desk on a quiet evening at home. This is the perfect setting for deciding what the best greeting style is for you. Look over what you did in the past or begin afresh today. Here are the most common favorites.

1. **The Traditional Holiday Card**
2. **An Electronic Greeting**
3. **A Holiday Photo Card**
4. **The Photo Letter**
5. **Social Media Greetings**

Opening a Thanksgiving, Christmas, or New Year's card during the holidays almost always brings a smile. You just have to decide on the best way to buy, address, and mail (or email) greetings more simply to keep it personally satisfying. What's your system?

1 The Traditional Christmas Card

Holiday greeting cards hold a front and center place of style expressed by your card choice. Collecting them in a basket or hanging them on a stairway is always a favorite for the receiver. But for you the sender this can be time consuming unless you find an easier way.

> **TIP: Christmas Card**
> Here are some simplifying tips to send Christmas cards:
>
> - Count the number of people on your list and buy those cards as early as possible, either in your favorite shop or online store. Gather stamps and return address labels, too.
> - Choose one type of card for the year to simplify the process and avoid confusing it with what you sent last year.
> - Choose a card that expresses your style as elegant, traditional, religious, or personal.
> - Simplify by printing your computer list of address labels.

Do a simple budget analysis of how much the cards and stamps will cost you. If it's more than you have or planned on, you might want to consider sending an E-Card greeting by email to many on your list. Hand delivering cards to family, neighbors, church, or work will also save you some postage. Keep a separate list of those you will hand deliver. Instead of a label, handwrite their name to make it personal.

2 An Electronic Greeting

You might be wondering if it's acceptable to email a Thanksgiving or Christmas greeting. The answer is "yes" especially if you send the greeting to the people you connect with all year by email. Others who mail you cards yearly are those you can still send regular Christmas cards to. It's just a matter of moving in the direction you are most comfortable with—mailed cards or electronic greetings. You could do half and half for a while until you make a final choice.

How does this work? Create a Distribution List in your Email Contact System titled "Christmas." Add names of people that you meet and want to stay in contact with so your list is ready to go. Do it throughout the year to keep it up to date and that makes sending the greetings even easier. Send the electronic email to yourself and "bcc" (Blind Carbon Copy) the list of people. Begin the greeting by saying, "Dear Family and Friend" or Dear Friend."

You might even keep a couple Distribution Lists labeled "Christmas-Family & Close Friends" and "Christmas-Friends and Acquaintances." This allows you to write a more personalized greeting to family and generalize it for the acquaintances that don't need to know about your personal life.

3 Holiday Photo Card

The simplicity and warmth of a photo greeting card is gaining popularity, especially with the younger set. Just pick your photo or group of photos representing your year, design a card online, push the button and almost instantly the cards will be ready to mail.

The benefits of ordering may outweigh the cost if you are short on time or have an especially busy holiday season. Just plan ahead to snap photos at a special event, on a summer vacation or at Thanksgiving. Look for those delightful moments you want to remember. Photo centers like a drug store, discount or online store can quickly create these cards for a reasonable price.

TIP: Photo Card

If a picture is worth a thousand words, this greeting is sure to be a winner!

- Pick a photo that reflects you and your life. Pick a casual photo if that is "you" or a recent event that you enjoyed.
- Consider a vacation photo while on your "Trip of a Lifetime."
- Keep everyone updated with a wedding photo of you or your kids.
- Include yourself, not just your children. Friends want to know what you look like, if you gained weight or dyed your hair.
- Choose a few key photos and make a collage photo card if you can't pick just one. This is good to feature each family member as well. Pet photos are acceptable as long as you are in the photo, too.

---

4 Holiday Letter with Pictures

When you want to express yourself in words and pictures, the easiest way is to create a photo letter, or family letter, with pictures and text. This serves double duty for mailing hard copy and it can be saved as a PDF to be emailed as well. Bingo! You only have to create one file and it goes out both ways.

Last year one of my assistants sent her first digital holiday greeting and the subject line announced "The Bendenellis have Gone Paperless!" The digital Family Photo Letter had some older relatives upset, so they quickly printed up some copies and mailed them. Any change in formatting has a few glitches initially, but are worth the transition in the long run.

Keep a notebook of these yearly letters and a file or notebook book for each of your children. It will be a treasure for you and your family as you read through the life changes over time.

For your Computer file, save it in a file called "Christmas" and label each year's letter beginning with the year so they fall in order such as:

2012 Christmas Letter	2012 Christmas Addresses
2013 Christmas Letter	2013 Christmas Addresses
2014 Christmas Letter	2014 Christmas Addresses
2015 Christmas Letter	2015 Christmas Addresses

5 Social Media Greetings

If social media is a part of your everyday life all year, you have a built in way to connect with all the people in your networks. Why not use this to send out your special holiday message?

Be creative and you will be delighted at the warm greetings coming back to you. Choose a specific date like the Friday before Christmas week.

The sky is the limit for topics. Send messages throughout the holidays of Thanksgiving, Christmas and New Year's. You'll be encouraged to hear great ideas from your networks of all the good and generous things going on in their world and yours.

Note: Be sure to set up your email message on "Vacation Hold" if you are away from the office. That in itself is a way to enjoy the holidays. In addition, studies have shown people are most productive the week before leaving on vacation. Wrap up loose ends and let people know the dates you'll be away from work.

Three Opportunities to Send Cards

Thanksgiving Greetings

Thanksgiving is a wonderful time to send out greeting cards, especially for businesses or people who find December is their busiest time of year. Thanksgiving cards are appreciated because they are the first cards received and read. It also shows others you planned ahead and it will be one way to simplify your own busy holiday season, too.

If you send business greeting cards at Thanksgiving, then you can send family and friend cards at Christmas. Only one list per holiday.

A card expressing gratitude shows a caring attitude by those who have year-end crunch deadlines.

Christmas Greetings

Christmas is the traditional time to send annual greeting cards. The Post Office recommends mailing cards and packages between December 10-15 for delivery in the United States.

Ideally the earlier yours arrive, the more time the receivers have to write back to you when they send theirs. Send early in the season and you'll get more feedback and notes from others.

New Year's Greetings

New Year's Greetings are acceptable especially if you didn't have time to prepare Christmas cards and plan to write and send them the week between Christmas and New Year's.

The only problem is counting on the post office to get them delivered in a timely manner since they are still busy catching up on Christmas mailings.

Also people are often away and won't be reading it until mid-January. But if this is your preference, then by all means send an inspiring New Year's card and focus on the new year instead of the past year.

How Long Does it Really Take to Do Christmas Cards?

Keep track of how much time to allow based on how long it takes this year. You save time and simplify by keeping a record.

Track Christmas Card Time

	Year	Date Started	Date Sent	# Cards	# Emails	$ Cost	Next Year Tips
1.							
2.							
3.							
4.							
5.							
6.							
7.							
8.							
9.							
10.							
			Total:				

Simplifying is all about keeping records and improving the system. It could be as simple as a computer document of address labels in Word or Excel.

Christmas Card Greetings

My Christmas Card List

Create a master list in pencil so you can update it. Or print a copy of your computer labels. Check off a name when you receive a card. The secret to a smooth season is to keep the list updated. Now you know how many cards and stamps you need.

Tip: Print a copy of your computer labels, insert it in this section of your notebook, and check off a name and address when you receive a card.

	Sent		Sent
Name _John Smith_ Address _222 Evergreen Terr._ _Springfield, MO 65806_ _615-555-2255 jsmith@holiday.com_	07 08 09 Received 07	Name _____ Address _____ _____ _____	 Received
Name _____ Address _____ _____ _____	Sent Received	Name _____ Address _____ _____ _____	Sent Received
Name _____ Address _____ _____ _____	Sent Received	Name _____ Address _____ _____ _____	Sent Received
Name _____ Address _____ _____ _____	Sent Received	Name _____ Address _____ _____ _____	Sent Received
Name _____ Address _____ _____ _____	Sent Received	Name _____ Address _____ _____ _____	Sent Received

What Do You Do
with Old Christmas Cards?

You can't save everything, so what do you do with old Christmas Cards? They can serve more than one purpose. Here are a few suggestions to repurpose them:

- Read one card each evening at dinnertime and remember fond memories of the sender or family.
- Cut off and donate the front of the Christmas card to a hospital or school the following year for crafts.
- Use the front of cards for your Christmas gift tags next year.
- Save the photo cards in either a notebook, file, or rubber banded for good, with the name and year marked on the back of them.
- Keep this year's Christmas cards until next year, while letting go of the prior year so only one year is saved.
- Read last year's cards for inspiration and warm memories before writing your cards this year.

If you can't complete addressing and sealing your cards in an evening or two, it's probably too time consuming. Set up a better system and keep it simple!

The easiest way to keep in touch with family, friends and coworkers is the simple holiday greeting card. Simple, yes, but complicated if you don't have an easy system to keep track of people.

Comments from Holiday Class Participants

*"The first thing I'm going to simplify for my holidays
is start cards early and write a letter."*
—Carmen D.

*"The first thing I'm going to simplify for my holidays
is one style card and start cards earlier."*
—Karen W.

"I learned to keep my Christmas cards simple and start early."
—Gail H.

*"The first thing I'm going to simplify for my holidays
is to remember to buy one design on a Christmas card each year."*
—Berni M.

10 Tips for Successful Photos
BY PENNY CROSSON, BEAUTY EDUCATOR

Planning ahead is one of the keys to sharing a holiday card greeting. Here are some tips that will make putting a family photo on your Christmas card easy.

1 **Take Photos Every Year.** Yearly photos alone make the best Christmas gifts. Life is about relationships, and annual pictures keep you in touch.

2 **Snap Them Any Time of the Year.** Vacation photos capture fun with the family. You can take them throughout the year and they're more playful than a posed photo taken during the stress of the holidays.

3 **Take Them Outdoors.** To prevent shading the faces, avoid shooting in direct sunlight or mixed light and shade. Slightly overcast skies are perfect.

4 **Take Them Indoors.** Choose a simple background without reflections from a mirror or window. If you have a hard time finding a good spot, take a close-up shot.

5 **Choose the Best Time of Day.** Afternoons or early evenings when everyone is well rested are the best times to take photos, especially if you have to get your family ready by yourself.

6 **Plan What to Wear.** Choose solid colors that draw attention to you and not to what you're wearing. Red is a popular color for the holidays, but it draws the eye to itself first and then to the subject. Avoid busy patterns and bright colors. Light colors look best if you have dark hair, and dark colors if you have light colored hair.

7 **Capture the Best Facials.** Look down without smiling on the count of "1" and "2." Then on the count of "3" look up and smile! You'll have an excellent result every time.

8 **Include a Pet.** Including your pet in a family photo is fine if is the animal is small enough to hold still for a quick shot. Too many variables can distract from the focal point, the people. Keep it simple.

9 **Remember to Have Fun!** Candid Christmas pictures typically look more natural, bring more laughs, and better capture the mood than posed photos. Leave the posing for the professionals.

10 **Don't Stress.** If time is running out, be creative. One year my kids' football team went to the playoffs. During half-time I put a Santa hat on each of my children, snapped a picture, printed some to place in traditional cards, and emailed many photo e-cards that year. It's never too late to send a greeting!

Penny Crosson is a licensed cosmetologist, beauty educator, and wholesale/retail product provider. She is a speaker and author of Daily Make-up with The Master. *She works with health & beauty professionals and everyday people, teaching private and group classes on skincare, make-up techniques, health and nutrition, and marketing. Penny lives in Heath, Texas, with her husband and has two kids in college. Visit **pennycrosson.net***

Holiday Greeting Cards

1. Simplify your holiday greetings by using the same system each year and put a date on the calendar when you will do them, say two to three evenings.
2. Plan two or three evenings or one weekend to complete the process and track how much it costs. Play your favorite holiday music to get in the mood or watch a holiday movie.
3. Print a copy of your address list to keep in a Holiday file or Holiday notebook. Check off those you hear from so you can easily review the list for next year.

Personal Reflection

1. My Holiday Greetings work best when I _____

   _____

2. What I like about Christmas Cards _____

   _____

3. What I'd like to improve about doing Christmas Cards _____

   _____

Holiday Support Group Discussion Questions

1. Share what greeting card system you use and how it works for you.

2. Share what date you plan to write your cards and send your greetings this year.

3. How do you involve your family or does it all fall on your shoulders?

4. Who or what is your inspiration for getting your cards out?

5. How do you balance the cost of postage/e-cards and how many do you send?

6. What's the best thing about sending Holiday Greeting Cards, either Thanksgiving, Christmas, or New Year's cards?

7. Something I plan to simplify about my holiday greetings is _____

   _____

   _____

4

Holiday Decorations

Get Decorations Up and Down Easily

*The things that will put you in a holiday mood quickly
are Christmas decorations, flickering candles, and holiday music filling the air.
Decorating your home for the holidays is one thing that lets you "feel"
the holidays and make your home warm and cozy, so start early!*

*I*f your decorations cause you more anxiety than enjoyment, it's time to simplify. This is especially true if you seem to leave more and more of them packed away each year. Put out the ones you really like, and thin out what you don't like as much. Give away a little each year. Soon it will be simple.

Keep the Decoration Timing Simple

Once the holidays are over, people often feel that Christmas ends too soon and down come the decorations. How do you overcome that short-lived time? By picking the same time to put decorations up every year, you will simplify the whole process of setup and storage. Here's a calendar guideline to get the most enjoyment from your decorations:

- **Thanksgiving Weekend:** Put up outside lights. Wait until December 1 to turn them on.

- **Week after Thanksgiving:** Put up Christmas tree and inside decorations. Donate extras.

- **Nightly in December:** Enjoy your lighted decorations all season. Snap photos of them.

- **Weekend after New Year's:** Take down your decorations, reorganize, and pack them away.

Limited time can cause you to postpone or skip the decorating component. But this can leave you disappointed. Don't give up, be strategic and simplify. Put up the decorations that matter to you and take them down when the season ends. You'll be storing decorations for eleven months of the year, so make the effort to get them up on time. Then you can fully enjoy them for the important four to six weeks of the holiday season. that matter to you up and take them down when it really counts. You're storing decorations for eleven months of the year, so make the effort to get them up on time. Then you can fully enjoy them for the important four to six weeks of the holiday season.

Get Started

Choose a three-day time frame, like Monday, Tuesday, Wednesday or Friday, Saturday, Sunday. The first day pull out the boxes and put up the tree, the second day decorate the tree and home, and the third day finish decorating and put the boxes away. Store household knickknacks in the decorating boxes until you bring them out again after putting away the decorations. You now have a wonderful, festive looking home in a short amount of time without extra clutter!

Organize Your Boxes

As you get started, see how much room and how long it takes to put everything out. If it begins to feel tedious, consider donating some decorations to a charity or newlyweds. If the items are sentimental, take pictures to remember them and then donate. Save the space and enjoy the memory.

Line up boxes in one location of your home to be emptied, say against the wall in the dining room. As the boxes are emptied, line them up on the other side of the room. Stay organized.

Motivation to Decorate

Dragging out holiday decoration boxes is generally not a highlight in anyone's season unless you are motivated. Some fun motivators include:

- Plan a Tree Trimming Party. Invite family and friends for pizza and Christmas cookies after helping you trim the tree. Food brings out your helpers and kicks off the season.
- Schedule a Holiday Party. Company coming is a sure fire motivator to get everything in place... and then you can enjoy it with them the rest of the season!
- Capitalize on Your Travel Schedule. If you plan to travel at the holidays, put up your tree, front door wreath, and a table centerpiece to enjoy each night before you go.

Girlfriend Help — A Personal Story

For several years I envisioned a garland of white mini lights gracing the traditional white railing of my new home. I pictured my traveling relatives walking in the front door to "oh and ah" over the magic that greeted them. But each year our holiday lights were put aside with some light bulbs out. My husband insisted he could fix them but never got around to it.

While he was away on a trip and the holidays were fast approaching, my girlfriend helped me stretch out the light strings to see what actually worked. Three were partial strings, but one long one would grace the stairway woven with the green garland I had picked up at the store. I had tried the hardware store "Command Strips" to hold it, considered nailing cup hooks in the railing, and even tape to hold it up. Nothing was working.

Finally, my friend and I put our heads together and devised gold ribbon bows on the posts and ties on strategic spindles to give it the graceful swag I had always wanted. We flipped the switch and congratulated ourselves on our victory! It was the best present (and three hours) my friend could have given me. I was satisfied I had upgraded one holiday decoration that year and my husband was happy he didn't have to be involved.

Trim Your Christmas Tree

Usually the Christmas tree is the focal point of all holiday decorations. If you have an artificial tree, write down directions for getting it up. If it's a real tree, time it right so it smells fresh for your holidays and comes down before the needles fall. Follow this plan and your tree will be in place and fully decorated in one to three hours.

1. **Tree.** Set up the best view. "Fluff" branches on an artificial tree by bending them to their fullness.

2. **Lights.** Place the lights strategically. If that is tedious for you, consider getting a pre-lit tree now or at the end of the season.

3. **Ribbons, Florals, or Garlands.** These are optional. Attach top to bottom vertically or in horizontal swirls.

4. **Ornaments.** Put your favorites up first and consider donating those you don't use.

5. **A Tree Topper.** This may be just the crowning touch to finish off your tree.

6. **A Tree Skirt.** This covers your tree holder, especially if you raise it by placing your tree on a box for more height. It also leaves more room for presents.

A recent poll showed most people take down their holiday decorations the weekend after New Year's. Since that's the case, be sure to get your tree and decorations up early, especially since they take up significant space the rest of the year.

Get Creative with Centerpieces and Mantles

Centerpieces on festive table runners, candles, and holly provide a focus for any table that will keep you looking forward to dinner each night in December. Eating by candlelight is one of the best ways to relax during what could be a stressful season — but not any more for you since you are planning your work and working your holiday calendar plan.

A fire in a fireplace is a definite mood setter. To decorate your mantel consider adding holiday nutcrackers, poinsettia plants flanking each side, or hanging stockings. No fireplace? No problem. There is a TV channel with a fire in a fireplace. Check your cable listings.

Upgrade This Year

Each year think about simplifying or improving one thing. You don't have to create a picture perfect setting all in one year. Do it gradually and you will enjoy one upgrade a year, whether it's your outside lights, your centerpieces, or table settings.

Treat yourself to something new and pass on the "old" to someone who may find it brand new to their setting. Remember to consider the storage size of what you are adding and remember your goal is to keep it simple and manageable to put up and down.

Four Storage Steps

Decorations will take your home from ordinary to festive in an afternoon or weekend. But why is it such a chore for many of us? The reason is simple—storage.

When you put your decorations away, that is the time you can simplify. Keep thinking about how you can improve the storage and retrieval system.

1. Box It—The boxes you use can simplify your decorating process. For instance, consider upgrading tattered cardboard boxes to plastic ones with lids. Before you purchase anything, measure the size of the space so you will have neat, stacked rows. Clear boxes are nice if you want to see what's inside and solid colors are a good choice if you don't want to see the holiday decorations all year long. Artificial Christmas trees and other large decorations should be stored in the box they came in.

2. Bag It — Bag decorations like wreaths with a platform of sturdy cardboard or a clean pizza box under them to keep their shape. Solid colored garbage bags or clear dry cleaning bags work to keep the dust out.

3. Label It — The secret to simplifying any storage is labeling! Label, label, label! Use a simple 3 x 5 card to neatly print what's in the box. Or number the boxes and keep a list such as the one below.

Let Box #1 be the first-to-open container with everything you want to use first to get you in the holiday spirit, i.e. front door decoration, table runner, special candle, holiday mugs, nativity scene, or holiday dinner plates. Whatever warms your heart.

☐ #1 = First to Open
☐ #2 = Front Door Decoration
☐ #3 = Outside Lights
☐ #4 = Christmas Tree
☐ #5 = Favorite Ornaments

☐ #6 = Optional Ornaments
☐ #7 = Holiday Table Settings
☐ #8 = Garlands
☐ #9 = Stockings
☐ #10 = Wreaths

4. Nest It — Find the best place to store your decorations while considering you are giving up eleven months of the year to storage. That's a good deterrent from buying more each year.

For easy access, store decorations together in locations such as a section of the garage, attic, under a stairway, or a corner of the basement. Store heat-sensitive items inside your home, such as holiday candles, CDs, and DVDs in a cabinet or closet you can access easily. Label the box.

Mostly you are looking for a safe place that's easy for the person putting up the decorations to access. If you need to cajole a husband, boyfriend, or son to bring the decorations down, then consider an area you can get to yourself. The stress of engaging someone else is sometimes not worth it. Become a "do it yourselfer" to simplify the process on your own time schedule, though warmly welcome any help with great appreciation.

Keep a Decoration Storage chart only if that simplifies your process. Put the containers away in reverse order by putting the ones you'll need last at the back and the ones you'll need first in the front to make retrieval easier next year. The important thing to remember it's easier to decorate if there is a repeatable system year after year. Keep it simple to enjoy it fully.

Decoration Storage

Box #	Label on Box/ Box Description	Contents	Location

Holiday Decorations for Your Holiday Photo Book

Simplify your decorating by keeping a holiday photo book of your decorations and any notes to make it easier next year. Soon you will look forward to seeing everything in place and know the most successful way that works at your home. Remember this is only one component of the holiday season so don't go overboard to stress yourself and others.

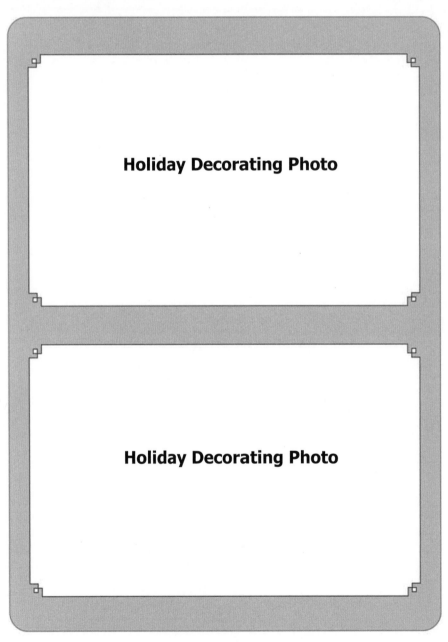

Holiday Decorating Photo

Holiday Decorating Photo

10 Tips to Decorate Your Holiday Home

BY KATHY MAYS, PRESIDENT KATHY MAYS CHRISTMAS DESIGN AND DÉCOR

Dressing up your home for the holidays can be as easy as 1, 2, 3. Simply turn on your favorite Christmas music and make some holiday hot cocoa. Lay out your favorite Christmas décor, slip into the holiday spirit, and decorate your home following these 10 simple holiday steps.

1 **Choose a Holiday Theme for Your Home.** Anything from a color or color scheme to a family tradition, toy tin soldiers, or nature itself will work. The choice is yours.

2 **Decorate the Front Door.** Wrap the front door frame with lighted garland. Add a nice wreath with festive ribbon and coordinating bow. Place on a gold or silver wreath hanger over the top of the door. Viola! The door is done and the holidays have begun.

3 **Change Your Everyday Doormat.** Add a festive holiday mat. Your guests will feel warm and welcomed as they approach your front door.

4 **Carry Your Theme Through Your Home**. Replace every day kitchen towels with Christmas towels. Add colorful Christmas balls to a crystal bowl or vase for a coffee table focal point.

5 **Replace Sofa Throw Pillows.** Trade out Christmas pillows in different sizes, shapes, and colors such as square, round, and bolsters. They can make interesting conversation pieces.

6 **Decide the Type of Tree You Want to Decorate.** "Focal Point Trees" are dressed in lights, ribbons, balls and florals. "Family trees" are dressed in lights with your family's favorite keepsake ornaments. Either one can be lovely.

7 **Coordinate the Fireplace Mantel and Your Tree Theme.** If you choose a neutral color theme, add a few colorful candles of varying heights in crystal candleholders. Then put clusters of Christmas balls to match the colors in your tree in a glass vase to give your mantel extra shine.

8 **Add Lighted Garland to Stairwell Railings.** Consider doing the same to your focal point window. All white light adds a touch of warmth, color and class.

9 **Make Your Homes Festive with Poinsettias.** You can add them to your entry way inside or outside, on a dining room table, fireplace hearth and throughout your home or outdoor patio.

10 **Top it Off with Your Favorite Christmas Scent.** Light a vanilla-scented candle or simmer cinnamon sticks on your cook top. Simple ideas like this make a holiday home.

Kathy Mays is Owner and President of Kathy Mays Design. Throughout the years Kathy has professionally designed & decorated residential homes and commercial businesses. She is an Allied Member of the American Society of Interior Design (ASID) and Certified Interior Designer in San Diego. Visit **kathymaysdesign.com**

Holiday Decorations

1. Simplify by deciding the dates when you will put up and take down your decorations.
2. Put decorations up early and donate or pass on to newlyweds or a charity anything you don't like or don't use. You'll be glad there's less to put away.
3. Take pictures of your decorations, including the tree, table centerpieces, front door, family room, and everything you decorate, to make next year's decorating easier. Save them in a holiday photo book or digital file.

Personal Reflection

1. To me, decorations are the best when I _____

   _____

2. What I like about my holiday decorations _____

   _____

3. What I wish would be different about decorating _____

   _____

Holiday Support Group Discussion Questions

1. What's a memorable experience you've had putting up holiday decorations?

2. Who enjoys the decorations the most?

3. What do you do to get the most from decorating but still keeping it simple?

4. Share what you usually do for putting up holiday decorations for Christmas.

5. When do you take your decorations down?

6. If you could change one thing this year about decorations, what would it be?

7. Something I'd really like to simplify about decorating is _____

   _____

> *Decorating your home for the holidays is one thing that can easily get you in a holiday mood. So get your decorations up early to fully enjoy them.*

Simplify Your Holiday Season

SECTION II
Places to Go

5. Event Planning Made Easy

6. Holiday Food — Keep it Simple and Impress Your Guests

7. Make the Most of Your Limited Time

8. Charitable Donations and Year-End Giving

The smell of Christmas cookies baking or turkey dinner with apple pie in the oven is sure to bring a smile to anyone's face. Mm, mm! Whether going to a holiday event or hosting your own, plan to make it festive with holiday food as you gather together.

5

Event Planning Made Easy

Host a Party at Home or Work

*Successful people do one special thing that other people don't do in their planning
—they begin with the end in mind. They think about what makes the holidays special,
and the answer is always "getting together with people."*

During the holiday season there are always "plenty of things to do and places to go" to get ready: shopping malls, online stores, and grocery shopping. But you can turn the tedious chores into fun times if you invite your favorite people over for a special event. Sure, you'll get together with family. But once you get your holiday plan into a working routine, you just might be able to reach out and gather some other people together for a memorable event. It could be a neighborhood party, a cookie exchange, office party, or an open house combining all three.

The holidays are all about taking time to honor the people we love and are thankful for throughout the year. Beginning with that goal in mind, keeps you focused on your plan. It helps you eliminate any unnecessary details that don't add purpose and value to your celebrations. .

Where Do I Find the Time?

I never thought I had the time to squeeze in an entertaining event until I attended one simple, amazing event. My new acquaintance, Ann Rahilly, had invited us to an open house on the first Sunday in December. That took preparation to kick off the season so early. What was also so unusual was that just the summer before, Ann's husband, who had been a doctor, was riding around the neighborhood on a Moped for relaxation, when he was killed by an oncoming car driven by an elderly lady. What a loss of husband, doctor, and friend.

So why did Ann host an open house in the midst of grieving through her first holiday without her husband? "I wanted my three girls (grade school and junior high) to connect with people and reach out to others. We baked lots of cookies together (which was a bonding experience), and we listed everyone who was meaningful to us. My family lives in Australia, so this get-together was particularly important to us since we didn't have family here for the holidays."

Ann and her daughters issued the open house invitation in one-hour time slots: neighbors from 2:00 to 3:00 PM, husband's work friends from 3:00 to 4:00 PM, and 4:00 to 5:00 PM for church friends. The mood was pleasant, the fare was tasteful, and the party was meaningful. No superficial display of holiday one-upmanship or showing off. Just a genuine gathering that said, "You're special to us and we're glad you came."

I learned that with a vision and a little planning, there was room to break out of the gift-shopping, card-sending, and house-decorating cycle and gather people together.

Who Do I Invite?

One of the best ways to begin is to think of groups of people who would enjoy being together. They could be:

1. Neighbors you say hello to but never have time to visit.

2. A reunion of people you traveled with this year on a cruise or overseas.

3. Coworkers from the office that could use some holiday cheer.

4. Your small group at church or your support group.

5. Walking partners that you see often but with whom you don't usually socialize.

6. Single parents and their kids who you see at school or sporting events.

7. Business vendors you deal with during the year.

8. Your best friends.

9. Your family, both immediate and extended.

10. Others: _____

Think about doing the event once, invite another person in the group to plan it with you, and get help from others to pull it off. Do the part you do best—food, invitations, or program—and let the others put their best efforts forward too. Everyone will enjoy contributing something they do easily, once you share the vision with them.

Three Questions to Begin Your Planning

Plan an event around three questions:

1. **What's your purpose?** Is it a neighborhood dessert night, a year-end office party, or the family Christmas gathering?

2. **What's your theme?** Is it a white elephant gift party, a neighborhood cookie exchange, or a musical theme with dinner before a concert?

3. **What's going to make it a good time?** Will you have door prizes, games, party favors, catered food, live music?

Once you answer those questions, you're ready to plan your event. Whether you are the host/hostess or a contributing member to an event, you will find it is one of the best gifts you give this year—open-door hospitality. It's rare these days, but it's also one of the best memories of the season. The joy shared will be felt the whole next year for the effort you extend. Everyone wants to be invited and included somewhere at the holidays. Let your friends know they're special to you.

Event-Planning Timeline

Check off the items below as you do them. Fill in your calendar.
Assign the tasks to specific dates on your holiday calendar.

Simply Start On Paper

Fill out an "Event-Planning Worksheet" for your event idea, Team Helper(s), and Guest List. Brainstorming on paper or with a friend helps get the ball rolling.

Schedule a date for your event after reviewing your personal calendar, work, school, community, and church events. This will become easier as you keep your holiday calendars over the years and note the traditional times for recurring events.

If you're planning more than one event, consider having them on back-to-back dates, such as a Friday and Saturday. Since your house will already be clean and ready, you can consolidate time and effort.

7–8 Weeks Before

- Make your list of names and addresses and get your invitations filled out.
- Look for trends in holiday decorations and food, such as current colors and recipes in magazines or online.
- Send out a "Save the Date" e-mail or postcard to attendees. Consider something like www.evite.com to include map directions and track RSVPs.

4–6 Weeks Before

- Send out the invitations.
- Finalize menu plans. Order bakery, store, or restaurant foods you will include. Gather recipes and stock up on ingredients.
- Gather nonperishable items, such as plates, napkins, decorations, party favors.

2–4 Weeks Before

- Plan party layout: agenda, table décor, games, food-serving stations.
- Borrow or rent food service items: tables and chairs, linens, serving pieces.
- Create setup and time agenda on paper.

1 Week Before

- Print menu and food preparation plan: when to pick up foods from restaurants or stores, when to make food items at home, and whatever else you think of.
- Confirm attendee count and e-mail a reminder with directions to the event location.
- Call your team of helpers to confirm their participation and let them know what time they should arrive.

Sample Event-Planning Worksheet

Event *Neighborhood Cookie Exchange*   **Date** *Sunday, December 12*

Party Idea

Theme: Neighborhood Cookie Exchange

Ask each guest to bring five dozen cookies. Package cookies in half-dozens and include a recipe for the cookies in each package. Ask guests to wear aprons. Invite at least fifteen guests so the variety of cookies will be wide.

After the party, put your copy of each recipe in this notebook.

Invitees

Leslie Evans, Jennifer Woods, Linsey Black, Jolie Lawson, Kelli Smith, Karen Richmond, Brittney Reid, Cassie Nelson, Tomi Carrington, Allison Rose, Jaclyn Hunter, Kim Kelly, Lara Rich, Mom, mother-in-law.

Save the Date: E-mail or send a postcard eight weeks ahead.
Invitations: Six weeks ahead.

Menu

Beverages: Hot Chocolate, Apple Cider, Coffee, Water

Food: Pretzels, spicy trail mix, gourmet cheese and crackers, tortilla roll-ups, finger sandwiches: pimento cheese, cucumber and cream cheese, and chicken salad.

Decorations

Table: Red mixing bowl (upside down) with cookie sheet on top with stuffed gingerbread men.

Other: Measuring cups with tea lights scattered around. Use baking tablespoons to stir coffee and serve Chex mix. Serve all food in mixing bowls or on cookie sheets.

Entertainment

Baker's Quiz—pass out ten-question quiz. Guests all take it, and multiple prizes are given out for most correct answers and most wrong answers.

Prizes: Magnetic measuring spoons for winners. Cookbook for most wrong answers.

When & Where

Sunday, December 12, _____
2:00 PM–4:00 PM, Come and Go
Karen's House: 1212 Elm Street
Your Town, State, Zip

Event-Planning Worksheet

Event _____   Date _____

Party Idea

Theme:

Invitees

Save the Date:
Invitations:

Menu

Beverages:

Food:

Decorations

Table:

Other:

Entertainment

Prizes:

When & Where

Sample Event-Planning Worksheet

Event *Office Christmas Party*   **Date** *Friday, December 9*

Party Idea

Theme: Office Christmas Party

All employees can bring one guest.
Maximum of 85 guests.

Invitees

All full-time employees in Accounting,
Production, Marketing, Human Resources,
Logistics, and Board of Directors

Save the Date: E-mail or send a postcard
three months ahead

Invitations: Six weeks ahead

Menu

Beverages: Punch, Coffee, Tea, Water

Food: Shrimp cocktail, salads, tenderloin,
whipped potatoes, asparagus, and bread.
Cheesecake and chocolate mousse

Decorations

Table: Large crystal rose bowls filled with
2 dozen red and white roses, each sitting on
a mirror with fresh green wreaths and
pinecones surrounding the bowl

Other: Tea lights scattered around. Small
vases with red and white roses with sprigs of
fresh pine branches and pinecones to fill the
vases.

Entertainment

Each department will have twenty minutes
to construct a gingerbread house out of the
given materials. Board of Directors will
judge. Prizes given for Best in Show and
Most Creative.

Prizes: Best in Show wins one day of paid
vacation for each team member. Most
Creative wins $50 gift card for each team
member.

When & Where

Friday, December 9_____
7:00—10:00 PM
The Office
110 North Street
Anywhere, ST 45709

10 Tips for a Successful Party
BY ELIZABETH TOOLEY, EVENT COORDINATOR AND FORMER IBM EVENT PLANNER

Successful events focus on creating lasting memories and building relationships. Look for ways to enhance the atmosphere and use your best resources of time, creativity, and community.

1 **Purpose Communicates Value.** Plan your party from start to finish carrying out the purpose of building community. A good plan takes parties and gatherings from mundane to meaningful.

2 **Make an Agenda.** Create a one-page agenda to capture all information, including a general party timeline, serving times and locations, and an activity schedule. Purpose, Plan, Action!

3 **Trends vs. Traditions.** New and exciting trends in colors and decorations can add fun and flair to any event. Traditions, on the other hand, are the familiar gatherings that warm our hearts and save time by doing what worked well before. Combine traditions and trends to create balance.

4 **Location, Location.** While your home is the most personal place to have any party, a community clubhouse or a private room at a restaurant can invoke a warm, personal feeling, too.

5 **Two Are Better Than One.** Invite a friend or family member to help shop, cook, and decorate. This cuts the time in half, doubles the creativity, and triples the fun.

6 **Theme Extreme.** For a cookie exchange use mixing bowls for centerpieces and baking sheets for serving trays. Create a party quiz about baking and recipe measurements. Give teaspoon sets, or cookie scoops for prizes.

7 **Sense of Community.** The most significant memories are created through joint experience. Have guests bring an item to add to the party theme or make one at the party.

8 **Dual Purpose Equals Simplicity.** Be creative and multifunctional to simplify your holiday party. Use party favors for décor, i.e. wire picture holders or small frames for place cards to take home.

9 **Buy in Bulk.** Great items to buy in bulk are invitations, paper goods, party favors, and serving pieces. Focus on your creative elements like games and décor.

10 **Review, Review, Review.** Use your Event-Planning Worksheet to record your favorite elements within three days of the event. Write down what worked and ideas for next time!

Elizabeth Tooley is an Event Coordinator for one of America's fastest-growing mega-churches. She served as an Event Planner for IBM for more than five years where she managed an employee benefits club of more than five thousand employees in six locations. She coordinates corporate team-building activities, including bi-annual golf tournaments and company-wide outings. Elizabeth and her family live in Fort Worth, Texas.

Event Planning Made Easy

1. Start your planning on an "Event-Planning Worksheet" for your event idea, Team Helper(s), and Guest List. Choose a date that's convenient for you and your team of helpers to get the ball rolling. Be sure to plan the food and entertainment, the two parts of a party.
2. Follow the Event-Planning Timeline or make your own for the coming event. Have people "Save the Date" to gather momentum and anticipation.
3. Enjoy the party, have someone take pictures, and clean up your notes the next day to make it easy to do from then on.

Personal Reflection

1. Events are best when _____

   _____

2. What I like about the holiday get-togethers is _____

   _____

3. One person I could host an event with would be _____

Holiday Support Group Discussion Questions

1. What's one of the best holiday events you've attended?

2. What made it so great?

3. Have you ever hosted an event for friends or family?

4. What was the best part about it?

5. What was the most difficult and how could you overcome it if you did it again?

6. If you could have your favorite group of people over, who would it be?

7. Something new I'd like to try _____

   _____

> *Capture the memory of your event with photos of the food, people attending and your team of helpers. Mail or email photos with a thank-you note right away. People love to be on a successful team and will likely be willing to do it again next year.*

6

Holiday Food — Keep it Simple and Impress Your Guests

Organize Your Holiday Menus, Recipes and Baking

The smells of turkey dinner with apple pie, or Christmas cookies baking is sure to bring a smile to everyone's face. Mm, mm! Capture your favorite recipes, menus, and a few table photos all in one place so it's easy to pull them out and create memorable moments.

One of the most celebrated traditions with a practical purpose is holiday food. The holidays become more festive with food, whether it's Thanksgiving or Christmas dinners, holiday parties, a neighborhood cookie exchange, or a workplace potluck. People are going to eat anyway, so why not serve their favorites and simplify the process for you?

From simple Party Mix to decadent chocolate dessert, you can keep your guests happy during the season. It just takes planning ahead and deciding what you want to do with the time you have. And there's always ordering out or "bring a dish" meals if you want to be free of kitchen duty.

Organize Your Holiday Recipes

To begin, pull together your favorite recipes and menus in a recipe box, a 3-ring notebook, or on your computer. If they are a part of your regular year-round recipes, make a copy and keep them with your holiday menus. If you find a recipe in a magazine or cookbook, again copy it and keep it with your holiday notebook or recipe box. Get organized to save time.

Save your annual dinner menus for Thanksgiving and Christmas, to remember what to put on your grocery list, when to thaw the turkey, and what favorite side dishes the family likes. By being organized you can be the hostess that everyone raves about.

Focus on the food to create a festive mood. Customize it from your own recipe box and keep notes from year to year to simplify your grocery shopping, cooking, and baking.

Get new ideas for traditional or brand new holiday menus and decorations by picking up a new cooking magazine such as Betty Crocker's "Thanksgiving Favorites," Martha Stewart Living's "Your Best Thanksgiving" or Paula Deen's "Christmas" collector's issue.

Update your Recipes

If it's been a while since you cleaned up your recipes, pick five of your favorites, and recopy or clean off the plastic holder in your recipe box. You can even create a tab called "Holiday Favorites" and start from there. Here are two samples to get you started.

From Lillian Reinertsen (Nana)   2 Hours//4 dozen

Christmas Wreath Cookies
Ingredients:

- 1 Stick Margarine
- 6 Cups Corn Flakes
- 30 regular sized Marshmallows or 3 cups Mini-Marshmallows or 3 cups Marshmallow Jet Puff)
- Red Cinnamon Drops
- Green Food Coloring

Melt the margarine and marshmallows together.
Add green food coloring to make it dark green.
Fold in 4 cups Corn Flakes.
Form wreaths quickly on wax paper on counter or cookie tray. While warm add red Cinnamon drops to give a Red Berry effect. Store in cookie tins.

From Sharon Jaynes   Make Day Before // Serves 6-8

Christmas Day Breakfast (or Brunch)
Ingredients:

- 1 pound of pork sausage
- 6 eggs
- 2 cups milk
- 1 teaspoon salt
- 1 cup of sharp cheddar cheese, grated
- 2 slices bread — cubed (remove the crust)
- 1 teaspoon dry mustard

Brown the sausages in a frying pan, drain all the grease, and set aside. Beat the eggs. Add milk, salt and mustard into eggs and stir. Layer the bread cubes on the bottom of a 9 x 13 baking dish. Then layer the sausage, followed by the cheese. Pour the egg mixture over the top. Cover and refrigerate overnight. The next day, bake at 350 for 45 minutes.

Keep your recipes organized so they are available any time you want to get started baking. Be sure to date each one and note where it came from as that might become a family tradition. There's always a story behind a recipe that you can jot down in a sentence or two.

Plan Ahead and Begin Your Baking

Look for ways to prepare food ahead and spread out baking and kitchen cleanup—perhaps once a week or weekend. If food is in your freezer to pull out on a moment's notice, you'll have more time to spend with your guests. Here are tips from Food Stylist, Jane Jarrell.

• Cookies

Bake cookies and freeze four weeks ahead. They stay fresh if you scoop them into balls first, place on a cookie sheet, and put in the freezer. Once the balls are frozen, place in a freezer bag and put back into the freezer. Using a permanent marker and write the date on the freezer bag to keep you current.

Store baked cookies in tins instead of plastic containers to keep them from going soggy. Place wax paper between the layers of cookies to keep them from sticking together.

• Cakes

Bake cakes three days ahead, cover tightly with wax paper, place in freezer bags, and refrigerate them. Remove from the refrigerator and add the frosting fresh the day of the party. Should you not have time to do a frosting, sprinkle with powdered sugar and top each slice with a fresh herb such as mint or lemon thyme.

• Nutbreads

Freeze nut breads four weeks ahead and keep them moist by defrosting them in the freezer bag. Remove from bag prior to serving so the top will not be soggy. Slice and sprinkle with powdered sugar or a cinnamon/sugar blend. Nut breads are terrific served warm topped with a caramel ice cream.

Organize Your Holiday Menus

What favorite foods does your family enjoy at the holidays? Every family seems to have favorite cookie and candy recipes passed down for generations. The women in our family know how to light up the faces of our family with Norwegian Krumkage cookies and thin, sweet pancakes called Tynepanakage for Christmas Day breakfast! Mm, mm! Add Sand Tarts and Christmas Wreath cookies for a dinner dessert and we are happy.

List your menus for the holidays or the week of the holidays for easy reference every year. Once you build your repertoire on paper, it will be a breeze to pull together a traditional dinner no matter how busy you are right beforehand.

Save yourself time and stress trying to remember what you serve with your traditional turkey or festive meal by writing out the entire menu including the shopping list. Snap a picture of the food on the table so you remember who was there, how to decorate, and even what you wore.

Keep photos of your festive holiday food pictures and captions (handwritten is fine) to jumpstart your cooking next year.

10 Festive Food Tips to Impress Guests

BY JANE JARRELL, DALLAS MORNING NEWS FOOD STYLIST

Holidays include socializing over good food. Pull out those favorite traditional menus and new recipes and give them a whirl. After all, it's Christmas only once a year!

1 **Plan Your Plate Presentation.** When planning a menu, a plate should look like an artist's palate with a variety of color. This approach will also assure you of a proper nutritional balance.

2 **Blend Traditional Favorites with a New Recipe.** Continue traditions by serving recipes from your grandmother's table. Also try something new that your family loves as you work toward creating your own taste traditions.

3 **Line Up Everything on One Counter.** Place all your ingredients, utensils, and pans in one area. This streamlines the process when you have everything you need prior to starting a recipe.

4 **Buy Good Quality Ingredients.** A dish can be no better than the quality of the ingredients it contains. Often the incremental cost of purchasing a better brand is nominal when you consider the quantity used and its impact on flavor.

5 **Accomplish Like Tasks Together.** To save prep time, assemble all of your ingredients first, then wash, dry, and chop. Keeping your activity in one place simplifies your movement around the kitchen.

6 **Line Up Your Food Platters Creatively.** Alternate heights, labels, and garnish with fresh flowers. Think eye appeal. Serve the platters so that they are easy for your guests to reach and enjoy.

7 **Think Eye Appeal.** Display attention-getting food platters on varying the heights of wrapped boxes or on different-sized boxes under a beautiful table fabric.

8 **Plan Your Buffet Display around Your Opulent Desserts.** Decorate the buffet with different types of cheesecakes, fruit tarts, and cookies placed on different levels or cake stands.

9 **Label Your Platters with Place Cards.** Let your guests know what they are about to eat and look forward to the experience. Embellish a platter with a small glass bud vase and single stem flower to coordinate with your colors.

10 **Try New Recipes.** Do a test run on new recipes prior to having company. Are the items easy to keep warm? Can they be made ahead? Are they good reheated? Does your family love them? If not, rethink the dishes.

*Jane Jarrell, a former emcee for Southern Living Magazine's cooking shows, has written fourteen books and co-authored over twenty others. She is a photo stylist and special contributor to the Dallas Morning News lifestyles pages plus a sought after speaker at national and regional conferences. She and her family live in Richardson, Texas. Visit **janejarrell.net**.*

Update Your Recipes

If it's been a while since you cleaned up your recipes, pick five of your favorites, and recopy or clean off the plastic holder in your recipe box. You can even create a tab called "Holiday Favorites" and start from there. Here are two samples to get you started.

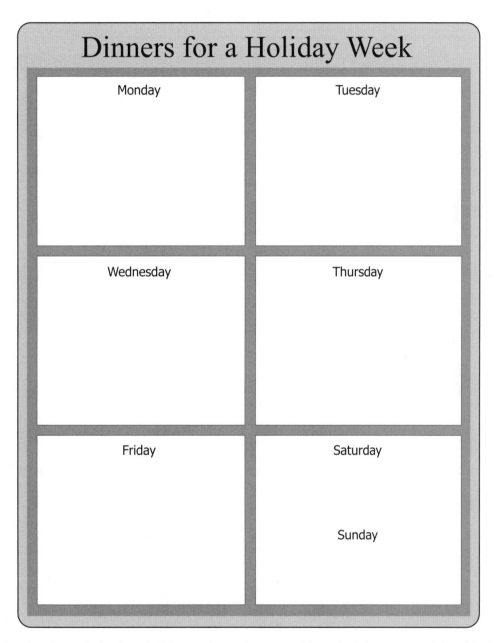

Dinners for a Holiday Week

Monday	Tuesday
Wednesday	Thursday
Friday	Saturday
	Sunday

Serving dinner during busy holiday weeks can be easy — if you don't have to spend time figuring out what to cook! Make those busy November-December weeks in the kitchen easier on yourself. Keep the meals healthy at home so you can enjoy eating when you are out celebrating.

Keep Your Holiday Menus

A traditional Thanksgiving or Christmas dinner often has the same components each year. A meal can create a family gathering everyone looks forward to. Make it special and fun. Here is an example of a detailed Turkey Dinner Menu from start to finish. Though there are a lot of items, it actually simplifies the process because everything is listed.

MENU	SERVING PIECE	GROCERY LIST
Appetizer: Juice & Crackers	Round platter & juice glasses	apple juice, crackers & cheese
Turkey (Put in at 10:30 AM) (5-6 hr. 325 oven)	Good china platter	20 lb. turkey 28 slices of bread
Stuffing with raisins	oblong bowl	1 cup onion, 4 cups celery
Mashed potatoes (45 min. 350 oven)	Round bowl & gravy boat	2 eggs, 4½ lb. potatoes, poultry seasoning
Green beans / corn (15 minutes)	Smaller round bowls	Butter and slivered almonds
Ribbon Jell-O salad	Clear bowl to show layers	Red, green, & yellow Jell-O
Jellied cranberry sauce	Small sauce dish	
Water, ice, milk, coffee, and tea		Milk, coffee, tea Sweeteners
		Centerpiece, candles, napkins
Festive dinner rolls (5 min.)	Basket with holiday cloth	
Apple and pumpkin pies	Holiday serving platter	Plastic wrap, aluminum foil
Ice cream or whipped cream	Salad plates	Pies, whipped cream, ice cream
Day Before: Set table; put out serving pieces and utensils; make dessert and salad; check drinks; clean kitchen, bathrooms, family room.	**Turkey Day:** Start turkey and potatoes, Chop vegetables.	**Helpers on Turkey Day:** Put ice into container, butter on tray, and arrange cranberries, appetizer, rolls ahead. Clean up kitchen.
Notes:		

10 Tips to Celebrate Without Gaining Weight!

BY DANNA DEMETRE, HEALTHY LIFESTYLE AUTHOR & COACH

1 **Drink a Large Glass of Water Before Facing any Food Temptation.** Water not only fills you up, but reminds you of your goal to eat with purpose at social events.

2 **Get a Reality Check.** Most holiday cookies, candies, and other treats are at least 150 calories per ounce. That's more than a full tablespoon of butter. If you eat 10 morsels, you could gain a half pound of fat at one party!

3 **Practice the Ten-Minute Delay Rule.** Every time you have an urge to eat one more goodie, make yourself wait ten minutes. If nothing else, you will eat considerably fewer calories by delaying.

4 **Stabilize Your Blood Sugar to Decrease Cravings.** A lean, healthy breakfast and lunch that each have at least 15 grams of protein and 5 to 10 grams of fiber (and no empty calories) will give you great energy and balance to withstand temptations more effectively!

5 **Burn More Calories Every Day.** Work off the extra calories you eat this season. If you add at least 30 minutes of aerobic activity each day, you could burn an excess of 3,500 calories or more between Thanksgiving and New Year's. That's one pound of fat!

6 **Stock Up on Healthy Snacks that Will Help You Say "No."** Avoid the goodies and treats that really aren't your favorites anyway. Healthy energy bars will give you a "sweet fix" and still keep you on track. Fruit, veggies, and nuts (in moderation) are always great options.

7 **Always Bring a Healthy Alternative to Any Dinner or Party.** That will allow you to eat a bit more volume of something you know will fill you up without all the fat or calories.

8 **Put On Your Bathing Suit Every Day.** Ask yourself in front of a full-length mirror this question: "Do I really want to store extra fat on my body this holiday season?"

9 **Change Your Self-Talk.** Start telling yourself daily truths that will change your neuron pathways and move you toward a healthier perspective, such as: "I am easily satisfied." "I enjoy being healthy and lean more than indulging in unhealthy foods." These messages repeated daily can actually change over time the way you respond to temptation.

10 **Remind Yourself You Can Have Anything You Want, Anytime You Want It.** You just don't need to have it all right now. Choosing to have a lean body that is full of energy is the best gift you can give yourself and your family this Christmas!

Danna Demetre is an international speaker and author, best known for her most popular book, Scale Down: A Realistic Guide to Balancing Body, Soul & Spirit. *She is a former radio host and a frequent media guest. She is the author and producer of healthy-self talk CDs that can help anyone develop a healthier mindset and reach their goals. Visit:* ***dannademetre.com***

Holiday Food:
Keep it Simple and Impress Your Guests

1. Enjoy your holiday season with the special foods that accompany any festivity. Simplify by organizing your recipes and menus.
2. Calendar your baking nights or weekend so you'll get ahead of the game.
3. Take pictures of your table and holiday food buffet and the people enjoying them in order to be inspired anew every year.

Personal Reflection

1. My holiday food preparation generally consists of _____

   _____

2. What I like about holiday cooking and baking is _____

   _____

3. One way I could make cooking easier on myself would be _____

   _____

Holiday Support Group Discussion Questions

1. What's one of the best holiday meals you've cooked?

2. What made it so great?

3. Do you involve family or friends helping out with the food?

4. What makes your Thanksgiving or Christmas dinners special?

5. What was something you learned the hard way?

6. What was the nicest thing someone said about your cooking?

7. Something I'd really like to simplify about my menus and recipes is _____

   _____

> *Holidays are all about eating and socializing over food. Often it's not just about the food, it's about the mood. So enjoy yourself and everyone else will, too!*

7

Make the Most
of Your Limited Time

Balance Your Time for Family, Friends, and Yourself

*Once you learn the secrets to manage the season successfully,
you will look forward to the best time of the year, every year
instead of getting caught up in the busyness of the season.*

The busiest time of the year descends right when we have the most to do! It is the wise woman who goes into the season armed with Time Management Tools to make the most of her limited time. Once you know how to manage your time, you can turn the seasonal stress upside down into holiday success. It just takes some insider secrets to do so.

Time Tools to Make Things Go Smoothly

In my landmark book, *Simplify Your Time: Stop Running and Start Living*, I share 101 Time-Saving Tips and a 30-Day Time Makeover. Let me give you a crash course for the holidays.

1. **Plan Everything on Your Monthly Calendar.** Keep everything for the holidays listed on your monthly calendar. You'll be neat and organized if you carry it with you. Or post the Holiday Season Calendar Plan on the refrigerator where you will see it every day.

2. **Write a To Do List Everyday of the Holiday Season.** This is the secret to accomplishing priorities each day in addition to the many little items that need to be done.

3. **Live in Peace and Harmony.** Keeping yourself calm no matter what comes up is one of the secrets to maintaining your balance at home and at work. Give up trying to control things out of your control, and don't lose your peace over a cranky clerk or unforeseen disappointments.

4. **Regroup When Things Go Wrong.** Stay flexible when relatives change their plans, a crisis arises at work, or things get tense at home. Determine to not lose your joy this season no matter what happens. There's a silver lining in every setback. Look for it!

Now let's take a look at your calendar and begin to customize your seasonal plan.

Calendar Tips
for the Holiday Season

	Monday	Tuesday	Wednesday	Thursday	Friday	Saturday	Sunday
8 Weeks ❏ Fill in Gift List ❏ Mark Calendar ❏ Wrapping Center							
7 Weeks ❏ Buy 1/3 Gifts ❏ Cards & Stamps ❏ Event Page							
6 Weeks ❏ Buy 2/3 gifts ❏ Wrap Gifts ❏ Write Cards							
5 Weeks ❏ Thanksgiving ❏ Plan Menus ❏ Use Friday Well							
4 Weeks ❏ Finish Gifts ❏ Finish Wrapping ❏ Start Decorations							
3 Weeks ❏ Decorate Home ❏ Address Cards ❏ Host Event							
2 Weeks ❏ Bake Cookies ❏ Clean Home ❏ Donations							
1 Week ❏ Enjoy Events ❏ Finish Bake ❏ Social Media							
Christmas ❏ Celebrate! ❏ Exchange Gifts ❏ Attend Services							
New Year ❏ Celebrate! ❏ Put Away Decorations							

Side tabs (top to bottom): Plan, Shop, Wrap · Mail & Decor · Celebrations

A Holiday Season Calendar Quiz
Things to Do, Places to Go, People to See

Take a look at your monthly calendar, much like the example here. Write in the dates when you will do the following. Cross out those items you are not going to do.

1. Do you have key holidays marked: Thanksgiving, Christmas, and New Year's? __Yes __No

2. Do you have work and school holiday vacations marked? (Highlight with color.) __Yes __No

3. Do you have the last day of work and school marked? __Yes __No

4. Do you have family birthdays and other special dates marked? __Yes __No

5. Do you have any personal travel dates marked? (Use a different color.) __Yes __No

6. Do you have social events listed, i.e. concerts, charity/religious events, etc.? __Yes __No

7. Do you have your Master Gift List and first shopping date marked? __Yes __No

8. Do you have dates marked to get your Christmas tree up and down? __Yes __No

9. Do you have target dates to start and complete your holiday greeting cards? __Yes __No

10. Do you have Christmas baking dates marked? __Yes __No

Do I Really Want to Be This Busy?

Now go back over your holiday calendar and ask, "Do I really want to be this busy?"
If the answer is "Yes, this looks fine," then post your calendar and move ahead.

If the answer is "No, it's too busy and stresses me out," then look for ways to selectively trim back the overload with these suggestions:

*   Limit the evenings out in a week. I recommend 3-4 at most, per normal week, though you know yourself best. The important "home time" allows for "downtime" when the pressure is off and you attend to normal weekly needs like kitchen cleanup, bill paying, laundry and family.

*   Prioritize events and let go of those that would "put you over the edge." Any one event is not the problem in itself. It's the accumulation of too many that wears us out.

*   Look forward to the holiday pace slowing down at work and school as Thanksgiving and Christmas approach. Everyone moves into their own world of family celebrations. It's nice.

Pockets of Extra Time at the Holidays

Believe it or not, there are weeks with extra time. Plan these weeks as downtime in your calendar to relax or catch up on life. These include:

- ## The Extended Weekend

   Thanksgiving Weekend. The three days after Thanksgiving Thursday allow for your personal choice: shopping on Friday (the busiest shopping day of the year), sleeping in, putting up holiday outdoor lights, or taking a deep breath and relaxing.

   Of course if you have children, these can be busy vacation days at home or away. But even children need a break from the pressures of their life. Just ask what they'd like to do and honor their requests. Offer suggestions and get a consensus of what a good Thanksgiving weekend would look like.

- ## Christmas Week Vacation

   Often Christmas falls on a weekday and companies and schools give the rest of the week off. If not, many workers are gone so it can be a nice time to take a break. Plan for this, eat lots of leftovers, and enjoy the time with family or close friends.

   If you find this time unpleasant or not to your taste, plan things to overcome that, i.e. like being with people you like, a trip away, new movies to watch or books to read. Again, planning is key. Know where your pitfalls are emotionally and build a bridge in a different direction.

- ## Last Week of the Year

   This is your "bonus week" of the year often between Christmas and New Year's Day, though sometimes the rest of New Year's week depending on what day January 1 falls on. Check it out and plan to clean up the house and holiday decorations while getting ready for the new year.

   This week consider What could I do to finish the year? Wrap up anything that would make you feel happy to get behind you. It's also a good time to clean up your desk, paperwork, email inbox, and organize financial papers or do any other tasks that would ease the pressure during your usual routine.

   It's true that holidays bring added stress. But it's also true that they provide a time-out from everyday life. Plan ahead and take advantage of the bonus time the holidays afford.

Ten Do's and Don'ts
to Simplify the Holiday Season

DO'S	DON'TS
1. Do stay ahead of the holiday stress by posting a holiday calendar plan.	1. Don't wait until you feel like it to get started.
2. Do modify the calendar plan to fit your personal plans.	2. Don't forget to write everything down on the main calendar.
3. Do look for weeks that are too full and will cause extra stress.	3. Don't agree to events that cause you too much stress.
4. Do look for things that you personally enjoy in the season.	4. Don't assume this year will be just like past years.
5. Do include a new activity that will help you get into the holiday mood.	5. Don't keep going to events just because you have in the past.
6. Do ask family and friends what they would like most to do this year.	6. Don't assume you know what others want to do. Ask them.
7. Do get your gift shopping, card sending, and decorating done early.	7. Don't wait on other people to get started.
8. Do contribute your time and/or finances to worthy causes.	8. Don't be a Scrooge and think of only yourself. Reach out.
9. Do encourage and help others who need help to get through the holidays.	9. Don't think others don't need help. Everyone likely does in some way.
10. Do be sensitive to others and make their holidays special by being kind and forgiving of stresses that arise.	10. Don't be demanding of others. Be a peacemaker everyone will appreciate.

Make the Most of Your Limited Time

Family Time

Eat as many meals together during the holiday weeknights and weekends as possible so you don't lose touch with those you love most. Minimize outside work and maximize family routines together to keep home stress to a minimum.

When you're doing the family Christmas cards, get an assembly line going. After you have addressed the envelopes, line up envelopes to stuff and stamps to lick.

Social "Friend" Time

Combine your limited social time by inviting friends to an event you are attending and meeting for dinner ahead of time or dessert afterwards. This combines two potential evenings into one and creates a memorable experience you will share.

Holiday Prep Time

Mark your calendar with two-hour appointments for Christmas preparations, such as Thursday, bake; Friday, decorate; Saturday, shop and wrap; Sunday, relax.

Company Time

Remember two key rules for successfully hosting family and guests during the holidays:

1. Keep them fed.
2. Keep them moving.

Also plan your meals ahead at least the night before, if not weeks before. Usually one bigger meal of the day so you only have a big cleanup once. Vary it with going out and accept the offer of your guests to take you out to dinner.

Stress Time

Enlist a holiday buddy to help you plan, especially one who is better in an area you are weak in. Bounce ideas off your girlfriend occasionally, but also journal to blow off steam instead of at an innocent clerk.

Personal "Me" Time

'Bookend' each day with time for yourself in the early morning and before going to sleep at night. Choose a holiday devotional book such as my Simply December Devotions for mornings and a novel to curl up with each night to get you through the season. By all means get your sleep! You need extra rest to handle stress.

Savor one event or daily conversation by jotting it down in a Christmas journal. Title it "*The Best Things That Happened to Me This Christmas*."

10 Tips for the Working Woman
BY GAIL HAYES, THE SUCCESS AND EMPOWERMENT TACTICIAN

The holidays can be a joyful time, but only if you make wise choices. Here are ten tips to help you "handle your business" and the holiday stress.

1 **Let Go of Unrealistic Expectations.** Missed deadlines and other negative events exist. If you focus on them, you will miss "joy moments" that accompany the holiday season.

2 **Do Not Over Obligate Yourself.** You are not the original Wonder Woman, but you are wonderful! Realize that you cannot be everything to everyone and if you must wonder, realize just how wonderful you are.

3 **Set a Deadline for When You will Stop Working.** Avoid working overtime. Prioritize your work, and when time is up, put on your coat, grab your purse and briefcase, and head home.

4 **Put Your Own Name on Your Gift Buying List.** It's okay to buy yourself a gift because you work hard every day. Make sure it is something fabulous and that it fits your budget.

5 **It's Okay to Ask for Help. Being a wonder woman is lonely.** There's something about the holidays that makes others want to be part of a team effort. Let coworkers pitch in to finish tasks.

6 **Take a Half Day Off and Watch a Good Movie.** The earth will not stop rotating if you take a break. Watch your stress diminish when you indulge yourself and relax during the holidays.

7 **Don't Forget Exercise, Self-Care, and Rest.** Exercise is one of the best remedies for managing stress. Swim, walk, run or ride a bike. Then set aside time for a bubble bath, your favorite nightgown, and go to bed early.

8 **Look Outside Yourself.** Take time with those who are less fortunate than you. It will brighten your holiday and give that extra boost of energy you've been searching for all year long.

9 **Make Contact.** Send cards to those who have touched your life this year. This will help build or maintain bridges for your business that you may need to cross in the new year.

10 **Read or Write that Book.** Relax and nourish your mind by reading and then journaling about your year. You'll be surprised at all you've accomplished.

Remember that your work is not your life and even Wonder Woman can experience the wonder of the holiday season!

Gail Hayes is the CEO of the Handle Your Business Girl Empowerment Zone where she leads women who lead women. She is an international speaker and author of the One Minute Success Secrets for Women, The Power of a Woman Who Leads, *and the* Handle Your Business Girl Empowerment Series. *Gail lives in the Raleigh/Durham North Carolina. Visit **drgailhayes.com***

Make the Most of Your Limited Time

1. Simplify by staying organized starting with your calendar. Every activity should be listed on your monthly calendar or our Holiday Season Calendar Plan.
2. Double check to keep weeks down to only three or four nights out at a time. Balance the many opportunities with your need to rest.
3. Enjoy the season by making the most of the "bonus" holiday days.

Personal Reflection

1. My holiday time works best when _____

   _____

2. What I like about the holiday time and want to be sure to include is _____

   _____

3. What people do you need to consider as you plan holiday events? _____

   _____

Holiday Support Group Discussion Questions

1. What does your holiday calendar look like — too busy or just right?
2. What do you notice once everything is in place for this year?
3. Is there something you'd like to change?
4. What would make it a restful and enjoyable pace?
5. How could you overcome some time obstacles?
6. What do you like to do on the bonus vacation days?
7. Something new I'd like to try _____

   _____

> *Remember you control your calendar. Very few events are requirements. Your calendar will be as full of festive events as you allow it to be. Choose those you want to attend and look forward to them. Let go of the rest.*

8

Charitable Donations and Year-End Giving

Give of Your Time and Talent

While we want to simplify the holiday season, it's also an opportunity to expand our generosity. Charitable giving shifts our focus from a personal gift list to the larger world around us. We can give time and finances easily if we plan ahead.

When we consider so many needs in this world, it is important to realize the holidays are an opportunity to make the most of reaching out to others. You can give of your time, talent and treasure. Financial year-end giving and donated items can both lower your taxes next year so don't put aside this important aspect of the holiday season. Both the holiday season and year-end giving converge. So how can you make the biggest impact by sharing your time, talent, and treasure without feeling stretched too far? This chapter will give you ideas and help fine-tune what you are already doing.

Why Donate?

"The amount of money and time that you, as an individual can give may seem small. But your donations added together, as part of a national—even global—giving movement, can make dramatic changes in the quality of life on our small planet," according to www.justgive.org.

According to the same website, the average American gives about 3.1 percent of his or her income to charity before taxes. That's well below the recommended 10 percent tithing level by religious institutions and allowed as an IRS tax deduction.

Surprisingly, individuals who give the most actually make the least. Households earning under $10,000 a year—far below the poverty line—gave 5.2 percent of their income to charity. That's a larger percentage of their money than any other income group.

Individuals give 75 percent of all the money that charities receive compared to 25% by, government or big corporations. As reported on justgive.org, "If we all give our fair share, no one will go hungry and no child will grow up in poverty."

Become a Year-End Holiday Giver

We may not be able to fly to Africa and help out, but there are several ways we can contribute to the needy right in our own area. It has been said that every one of us is touched by a non-profit in one way or another. That includes charitable organizations locally and globally, homeless shelters, hospitals, and even schools. So where do we begin?

How to Get Started Giving

Ask these questions to begin determining a giving plan.

1. What tugs at my heart: starving children in third world countries, a cancer research group, an animal rescue shelter, or the local rescue mission?
2. Who have I given to out of guilt just because a telemarketer called?
3. If I could choose one place to give my money and time resources, where would they go?

Qualities of an Ideal Volunteer

If money is tight, you can always volunteer your time. Every organization can use an extra pair of hands at the holidays. Together a group of volunteers can accomplish so much more. Your time is probably best spent with an organization that already knows the community needs and will be there to follow up once the holidays are over, rather than launching out on your own.

Be an ideal volunteer for any charity with the following qualities:

- Show up, suit up, and do anything needed!
- Adhere to the organization guidelines.
- Be dependable and a good team player.
- Be self-motivated without need for continual guidance.
- Be teachable and follow the organization's rules.
- Listen to the leader's guidelines for appropriate behavior with the clientele.

Often the needy people you are serving, known as "clientele," have been hurt by people who say they really care about them, but are just there to feel good about themselves. Be careful not to promise something even in passing that you will not follow through on. People remember. Be dependable and wise in what you say.

If you have $25 to donate, would you choose to give some to five organizations or the total to one organization? Considering the cost of mailings, flyers, administration and an office space, it is probably best to give to one organization. Go "deeper" instead of wider.

Spread Holiday Cheer through Charities

Donate your monetary and material treasures.
Advocate with your talents and be a spokesperson.
Participate by giving your time as a volunteer.
Invest throughout the year.

Make it a habit to donate regularly, advocate and volunteer at least three times a year. Remember charities need your help all year long, not just during the holidays.

3 Kinds of Charitable Givers

Consider where you might be in your year-end giving. Are you generous to everyone or closed off from all charity appeals? It can be anyone from the Salvation Army bell ringer to the stack of year-end pleas in your mail box. Here are three stages to consider where you are and how to best use your time.

Big-Hearted Impulsive Giver

Emotional giving is nice when someone knocks at your door or calls you on the phone, but how about giving because you planned? Some examples to begin using your big heart in a new way include:

- Donate time to serve a meal(s) at the holiday season.
- Help pack shoe boxes to send needy children their only Christmas gift.
- Find a local charity toy drive and purchase toys to give the kids.
- Decide as a family or group of friends to volunteer together.

Big-Hearted Intentional Giver

Year-end solicitations can fill your mailbox, so do collect them and give intentionally. Knowing charities depend on your year-end giving to meet the many people they help, this is one important time to give. Consider these options:

- Give 5-10% of your total Christmas gift budget to a charity of your choice.
- Go "deeper" into one organization rather than spread your donations widely.
- Start a chart and keep track of your giving and steadily increase it.
- Choose a charity and stick with it for the coming year.

Big-Hearted Committed Giver

Committed givers use holiday giving as a springboard for decisions for the next year. Giving monthly or quarterly in the coming year can take the stress out of adding charitable giving of time and finances during the holiday season. Some things to consider include:

- Donate time quarterly or monthly to the charity you serve holiday meals to.
- Use automatic bank withdrawal payments to your charity all year.
- Decide who to give to in the coming year and long term.
- Stretch yourself to give beyond last year or to reach the 10% deductible rate.

Wherever you are in your year-end giving, be a cheerful giver. It will be a "win-win" situation for you and those you give to.

Charitable Giving

To keep track of the many requests you will receive, keep a record of what you generously donate locally, nationally, or internationally. It is the season of giving, and many people are in need of help.

#	Charity	Year	Year	Year	Year
1	Name _____ Address _____ _____ Phone _____ Website _____				
2	Name _____ Address _____ _____ Phone _____ Website _____				
3	Name _____ Address _____ _____ Phone _____ Website _____				
4	Name _____ Address _____ _____ Phone _____ Website _____				
5	Name _____ Address _____ _____ Phone _____ Website _____				

Charitable Donations
for the Year

Your Name: _____ Year: _____
Address: _____ City: _____ State: ____ Zip: _____

#	Date	Charity	Total Bag/ Box	Amount
1.		Your Name: _____ Address: _____ City: _____ State: ____ Zip: _____ Phone: _____ Website: _____	# _____	# _____
2.		Your Name: _____ Address: _____ City: _____ State: ____ Zip: _____ Phone: _____ Website: _____	# _____	# _____
3.		Your Name: _____ Address: _____ City: _____ State: ____ Zip: _____ Phone: _____ Website: _____	# _____	# _____
4.		Your Name: _____ Address: _____ City: _____ State: ____ Zip: _____ Phone: _____ Website: _____	# _____	# _____
5.		Your Name: _____ Address: _____ City: _____ State: ____ Zip: _____ Phone: _____ Website: _____	# _____	# _____
6.		Your Name: _____ Address: _____ City: _____ State: ____ Zip: _____ Phone: _____ Website: _____	# _____	# _____
7.		Your Name: _____ Address: _____ City: _____ State: ____ Zip: _____ Phone: _____ Website: _____	# _____	# _____
		TOTAL DONATIONS	# _____	# _____

Itemized List
for Charitable Donations

Your Name: _____ Year: _____
Address: _____ City: _____ State: _____ Zip: _____

#	# of items	ITEM DESCRIPTION	@ $ Amount	$Total per Line
1.			$	$
2.			$	$
3.			$	$
4.			$	$
5.			$	$
6.			$	$
7.			$	$
8.			$	$
9.			$	$
10.			$	$
11			$	$
12.			$	$
13.			$	$
14.			$	$
15.			$	$
16.			$	$

Dropped Off?_____Picked Up?_____ Total Bags_____ Total Boxes_____

Chart courtesy of Marcia Ramsland • www.OrganizingPro.com

10 Tips to Spread Holiday Cheer

BY KAREN CLARK, NON-PROFIT PROFESSIONAL AND ADVOCATE

1 Be a Volunteer. Head to your local food bank or homeless shelter to serve a meal or do a community project. Find a charity you like and help during their busy holiday outreaches.

2 Clean Out Your Closet. Year-end clothing donations help both you and the recipient in a big way. You get a clean closet and the thrift store finds the perfect person for your clothing, towels and bedding. Finish the year with a tax receipt for your efforts, too.

3 Party with a Purpose. At your holiday event have guests bring a gift card, new socks or mittens to give to a homeless shelter. Or bring non-perishable foods for a local food bank. Focus on one. Afterward thank the guests with a final tally of their impact together.

4 Advocate by Speaking Up. Your work, school, church, or neighborhood is often looking for a project to focus on. Speak up for a need you know of in an organization of your choice.

5 Search for a Good Charity. Check out a list of charities, rated and centralized, at **www.greatnonprofits.org**, **www.charitynavigators.org** or **www.guidestar.org**.

6 Share through Social Media. In just seconds become a "Fan" and ask friends to "Like" your favorite charity's Facebook page. Spread the word why it's a great group.

7 Teach Kids to Give, Save, Invest, and Spend. Help children learn the art of giving their time and money as well as donating clothing and toys to kids in need.

8 Give Donor Gifts to Family and Friends. Purchase a gift card through www.justgive.org and let the recipient pick the charity it goes to. Or buy a sheep, books, water purification, or mosquito nets to help the third world. Example **www.oxfam.org**.

9 Raise Money. Shop, sell, or donate for a good cause on eBay at givingworks.ebay.com. Offline do a walk-a-thon, car wash, pancake breakfast, or special fundraising event.

10 Consider Giving Online. The average online donor gives between 10 a.m. and noon, 96% have made donations in the past, and they are likely to give in December. The average online donor is 38 years old while those 60+ years old give offline. Both are needed!

*Karen Clark is a nonprofit professional and has many years of experience in leadership and expansion of the visibility of organizations and generating substantial additional resources. She is a persuasive advocate for the not for profit community and believes investing in the lives of others is an investment for our future. She lives in San Diego. Visit **friendraisertoday.com***

Donations and Year-End Giving

1. Simplify the barrage of year-end donation requests by putting together a plan of who and what you are committed to. Keep a hard copy or digital list with your financials for reference.
2. Remember an extra pair of hands really makes a big difference for non-profit organizations and eases the pain of life for the recipients.
3. Consider using your holiday season donations as a springboard for commitment for the coming year. Once you organize your giving patterns, you can donate spontaneously as well.

Personal Reflection

1. My charitable donations feel most rewarding when _____

   _____

2. What I like about the holiday charity options is _____

   _____

3. One non-profit organization doing the work I really believe in is _____

   _____

Holiday Support Group Discussion Questions

1. What's one of the best "time" donations you've made at the holidays?

2. What made it so great?

3. Have you ever served a meal at a rescue mission or shelter at the holidays?

4. What was that experience like?

5. Do you feel best about contributing time, household goods, or finances and why?

6. If you could change one thing in the world, what would it be?

7. Something new I'd like to try _____

   _____

> *A satisfying donation is a "win-win" situation for both you and the organization or individual you give to. Why? Because it feels good to you and ultimately meets someone else's need!*

Simplify Your Holiday Season

SECTION III
People to See

"Things to do, places to go, people to see"
is often our holiday mantra, and it always ends up saving
the best for last—people to see. Plan so you can enjoy opportunities
to be together without a lot of fuss.

9

Thanksgiving and the Extended Weekend

Bonus Time during Thanksgiving Week

Thanksgiving is the official kick-off to the Thanksgiving-Christmas-New Year's holiday season, which can set a positive tone for the rest of the year. Being thankful is good for your health, and a memorable meal with family or friends can improve and build stronger ties. It just takes a little planning ahead.

Three Elements for a Successful Thanksgiving Day

There are three simple elements to a Thanksgiving Day celebration and you can cover them quickly. With your notes organized for this year and thereafter, each Thanksgiving can become easier.

1. Invite Your Guests. Everyone loves to be invited even if they know they always go to "Mom's" house for Thanksgiving. Call or send an Evite to get people excited about the coming get-together. You can find out what they most enjoy about being together (a food or activity) and be sure to include that in your plans.

2. Plan a Great Meal. List your cooking times so you know how early (or late) you can sleep in on Thanksgiving Day and still get your turkey in the oven and serve dinner on time. List cooking times by making notes for a traditional meal, invite others to bring their specialty side dish or dessert, and you've simplified the day. Also plan a lighter brunch or supper so people stay cheerful as they wait for the big meal of the day.

3. Plan an Activity. This can be as simple as a guided "Table Talk" question in this chapter or as traditional as the morning Macy's Parade on TV or football in the afternoon. Others may help at a soup kitchen during the morning preparations. Or call on a family member who is alone or living in a nursing home.

Be aware of what pleases your guests. And if you are the guest, offer to come early to help, or delight the hostess with a floral centerpiece to show your appreciation.

Above all, be flexible and cheerful. No one likes a grumpy guest or time-driven executive on this relaxing holiday. Get enough sleep and plan ahead to be a welcoming hostess. They will be thankful they came to your house or that you were an appreciative guest at theirs.

Finally, take snapshots of serving your food creations and soon you will have your own photo cookbook of good food, table settings, and accessories to breeze through next year's Thanksgiving meal. It does take work, but with good planning you can leave out the stress.

Our Traditional Dinner

Create your own menu to include family food traditions and recipes to enjoy year after year.

Serving Time: **# People:**

MENU	SERVING PIECE	GROCERY LIST

Day Before:	The Day:	Helpers on The Day:

Notes:

Sample Turkey Dinner

This is a sample menu suggestion to use to create your own menu on the next page. A meal can create a family tradition everyone looks forward to each holiday. Make it special and fun. This sample menu for Thanksgiving or Christmas serves eleven adults and three teens.

MENU	SERVING PIECE	GROCERY LIST
Appetizer: Juice & Crackers	Round platter & juice glasses	apple juice, crackers & cheese
Turkey (Put in at 10:30 AM) (5-6 hr. 325 oven)	Good china platter	20 lb. turkey 28 slices of bread
Stuffing with raisins	oblong bowl	1 cup onion, 4 cups celery
Mashed potatoes (45 min. 350 oven)	Round bowl & gravy boat	2 eggs, $4\frac{1}{2}$ lb. potatoes, poultry seasoning
Green beans / corn (15 minutes)	Smaller round bowls	Butter and slivered almonds
Ribbon Jell-O salad	Clear bowl to show layers	Red, green, & yellow Jell-O
Jellied cranberry sauce	Small sauce dish	
Water, ice, milk, coffee, and tea		Milk, coffee, tea Sweeteners
		Centerpiece, candles, napkins
Festive dinner rolls (5 min.)	Basket with holiday cloth	
Apple and pumpkin pies	Holiday serving platter	Plastic wrap, aluminum foil
Ice cream or whipped cream	Salad plates	Pies, whipped cream, ice cream
Day Before: Set table; put out serving pieces and utensils; make dessert and salad; check drinks; clean kitchen, bathrooms, family room.	**Turkey Day:** Start turkey and potatoes, Chop vegetables.	**Helpers on Turkey Day:** Put ice into container, butter on tray, and arrange cranberries, appetizer, rolls ahead. Clean up kitchen.
Notes:		

10 Tips to "Table Talk" for Thanksgiving

BY BRENDA LAURENCE, WRITER AND SPEAKER

One of the most important things to keep in mind while planning your meal is that no matter how lavish or simple the food, your guests will remember the dinner conversation and mood of the day. A Table Talk question is a guide to help you be intentional about creating a positive mood as well as a memorable meal. Along with planning the other elements, add a conversation recipe to the menu by planning a Table Talk question.

Choose 1, 2, or 3 questions below to cover or put them all in a basket and let each person draw one to answer. Usually these are best toward the end of the meal. Start first yourself to model what you are looking for.

1. What happened this past year that you're very thankful for?

2. Who are you thankful for that made a difference in your life this year?

3. What are you thankful did not happen?

4. If you were in a Thanksgiving play, what character would you be and why?

5. What is your favorite way to spend the day after Thanksgiving?

6. Medical science has proven that people with an attitude of thankfulness are healthier and live longer. What helps you to be thankful all during the year?

7. What is your favorite dish in the Thanksgiving meal?

8. Everyone is thankful for laughter. Share a humorous Thanksgiving memory.

9. The Pilgrims paid a tremendous price, and many died to establish the freedoms in of our country. How has their quest for freedom enriched your life?

10. What are you hoping to be thankful for this time next year?

Thanksgiving is a time to be thankful. Mixing fun conversation about the first Thanksgiving Day with expressions of individual thanksgiving will create an atmosphere of warmth and heartfelt thankfulness. If one person goes deeper in their reflection, then others do. Each year is a new experience and worth the risk.

Brenda Laurence is a speaker and author of numerous magazine articles and small group curriculum. She is passionate about strengthening relationships in couples, families and friends through home entertaining and meaningful conversation. Brenda and her husband are founders and authors of Encounter Marriage Weekends. Visit **encountermarriageweekend.com**

The Thanksgiving Extended Weekend

The Thanksgiving four-day weekend can be considered "bonus" time since it is a longer weekend. Look forward and plan this as downtime in your calendar to relax, catch up, or spend more time with family. So what can you do?

Thanksgiving Friday

Usually considered "Black Friday" by merchants who know this is the biggest shopping day of the year, stores offer sales and enticements to get people into their stores. Many shoppers delight in rising early to be one of the "first 100 shoppers" to get their bonus. And now online stores are capitalizing on this day without people even having to leave home.

Friday and Saturday are great days to work on your Master Gift List shopping, get holiday card addresses together, or put up outside lights while you have "man power" to help. They are also days to create a family memory by going to a museum, shopping for kids or spouses, or attending a play or movie together. Create a memorable family activity that everyone enjoys.

One family I know goes shopping with their teenagers that day. The teens go to their favorite stores to try on clothes and leave them "on hold" before telling their moms what they found and like. Their mothers can then stop at those stores and buy their Christmas presents early. The teens are still surprised when they open the very items they selected!

Thanksgiving Weekend

For many people the four-day Thanksgiving weekend can be a time to travel to s[...] resort or ski vacation. The planning ahead to get plane tickets and hotel arrangement[...] get away. It's like a mini-vacation before the busyness of the end of the year.

One of my friends annually plans a Family Reunion from Thanksgiving Wednes[...] for 35-40 cousins, their families, and two aunts in San Diego. Most can drive in or st[...] They "hang out," talk and share, golf, bowl and walk the beach. They find it's easier to gather together on Thanksgiving weekend than at Christmas.

Thanksgiving Week

Taking vacation days early in the week of Thanksgiving works well because then you have the entire week free of work and school.

My husband and I have married children who alternate Thanksgiving and Christmas weeks with us. That way the family plane ticket expense is for one holiday week instead of two, depending on the year.

I learned long ago that the important thing about the holidays is to be together. So we have celebrated Christmas at Thanksgiving week because those loved ones are with us in person. We put up a focal point tree of gold and rust-colored ornaments and decorations to blend the two holidays in the same week. Thanksgiving was celebrated on Thursday and Christmas was on Friday before kids and grandkids flew home.

Thanksgiving Week (Sample)

Thanksgiving Week—First year celebrating Thanksgiving and Christmas with grandparents from Florida and daughter and husband from Chicago. We couldn't be together at Christmas, so we celebrated both holidays that week.

Sat.	Sun.	Mon.	Tues.	Wed.	Thurs.	Fri.	Sat.	Sun.
Nana and Erling here from Florida	Church Palm Springs 5 PM Cedar Creek Early Bird Dinner	Palm Springs Time Share for the day	San Diego Visited Lisa at work and condo shopping	Shopping and fun together Game Night	1 PM Turkey Dinner 7 PM Amarette and Erik's New Home for Dessert	7 AM Brian, Christy, Mark to parade Women: shopping Men: put tree and lights up	Nana's Coffee-cake 4 PM Christmas dinner 7 PM Christmas gifts 11:00 PM B & C Flew Home	Church Grilled Salmon dinner Game Night

Another way to share thankfulness is to have place cards say 3 x 5 cards folded with a Thanksgiving sticker and the person's name on them. Between dinner and dessert ask the group to write two things they are thankful for this past year inside the place card and then share aloud. Personally we save these each year and thumb through the ones from before to chuckle or reflect on how we've been blessed over time. It's inspiring!

10 Tips for Holiday Tablescapes
BY SUSAN WELLS, THE DECORATING COACH

Spruce up any holiday event with a beautiful table setting known as a Tablescape!

1 **Organize Complementary Colors.** Dishes, candles, tablecloths and accessories can be used for all occasions. Record items on computer, using a chart and photos for easy retrieval later.

2 **Create a Tablecloth Wardrobe.** Purchase colorful or patterned discounted lengths of fabrics (easy-clean polyesters that look like satin, cotton, chenille and more.) No need to stitch edges.

3 **Broaden Your Horizons.** Imagine how your dishes would transform against a red checkered cloth, fall paisley prints, or festive shimmering silver. Layer dishes over thematic table cloths, runners, or napkins. Old plates take on new looks next to different textiles and textures!

4 **Vary Old Settings.** Incorporate new color combinations. Instead of the same old grouping, envision various shades of white/cream, silver/blue, or red/gold. Mix patterns and plains, go entirely neutral, or throw in just one splash of color for a dramatic effect.

5 **Mix and Match.** Update or change the theme of your old dishes with new side plates or bowls from a discount store. Create endless seasonal looks with fresh splashes of red, blue, green. Side plates transform the appearance of your table from casual to formal.

6 **Convert Vegetables and Fruit into Holders**. Carve out an apple and insert a tea light, scoop a melon and fill with relish or condiments, hollow oranges or lemons and garnish with a single blossom. Display over leaves or holly and set in groupings along the table.

7 **Class Up Your Chairs.** Wrap a wide ribbon or length of fabric to the backs. Shape into a festive bow. Insert dried leaves, sprigs of fir, or Christmas tree baubles. It'll be the 'wow' factor that dazzles your guests as they enter the room!

8 **Renew and Restore.** Spray paint tarnished, outdated pieces such as trays, holders, or candle bases with new colors. Transform dull items into metallics. You can re-invent them each season.

9 **Layer Dishes.** Elevate the eye by inverting a bowl to bump up a relish tray or candle, add height to a platter cover with a bed of boughs. Congregate candles for more impact— votives with pillars, enhanced with tall candlesticks.

10 **Bring on the Bling.** Embellish tables with shiny, reflective "table jewelry." Draw the eye to dazzling festive items: a silver ribbon around cutlery, gold ornaments filling a crystal bowl, metallic wrapping paper as a table runner. Show off with touches of light.

Susan Wells, decor specialist and popular speaker, has enthused and amused audiences with her message, "Taste Can be Acquired, Style Can be Learned." She is author of "The Art of a Beautiful Holiday Table" *and other "How To" decorating products. Susan inspires women to make both heart and home beautiful. Susan lives in Toronto. Visit **thedecoratingcoach.com***

Thanksgiving and the Extended Weekend

1. Simplify your Thanksgiving meal by planning cooking times, letting others bring a side dish, and planning an activity. As a guest, offer to help and bring a food dish.
2. Plan Friday and the extended weekend to be a step ahead into of the holidays by shopping, relaxing, or putting up outside decorations with the "man power" that might be available.
3. Ask the family what they'd like to do and honor their requests. Build good times together.

Personal Reflection

1. One of my favorite Thanksgivings was when _____

   _____

2. My Thanksgiving menu consists of _____

   _____

3. We celebrate our Thanksgiving by _____

   _____

Holiday Support Group Discussion Questions

1. What is one of your favorite Thanksgiving memories?

2. What made it so great?

3. Do you have any funny Thanksgiving experiences?

4. What do you like to do on Thanksgiving Friday?

5. What do you like to be sure to do on the four-day weekend?

6. If you could change one thing about Thanksgiving, what would it be?

7. Something new I'd like to try _____

   _____

> *One year we received a Thanksgiving greeting card from a financial planner that caught my interest. It included a photo of the staff in a downtown inner city classroom seated among the smiling inner city kids. It showed they really cared about the community and they were thankful for their clients. It was touching.*

10

Christmas is Here!

Inspiration for Christmas Eve and Christmas Day

Christmas is here! What an exciting time of year to celebrate! There is a natural joy on Christmas Eve anticipating Christmas Day. Wherever you celebrate or however many family events you attend, each one is unique because of who attends and what happens. And each year is different so savor the moments.

How Do You Celebrate Christmas?

Now that the long-awaited day is here, how do you spend the day? Everyone I've asked has a pattern for celebrating Christmas. It's fun to ask your friends how they are celebrating and find out how unique your family is. Also to pick up some new tips to add something special. Here are some suggestions for celebrating Christmas Day:

Christmas Morning Celebrations

Opening Christmas presents is probably the most universal favorite activity of the holidays. The excitement of getting up early (or sleeping in) and gathering around the Christmas tree lets everyone feel like a child again on Christmas morning.

Either open the gifts all at once, or take turns opening one at a time from the youngest to the oldest so everyone can see the gifts and know who gave them. Then continue around the circle until all presents are open. This keeps everyone focusing on one gift and one person at a time. It's fun to watch people "ooh" and "aah" over each one, and it spreads the time out and extends the joy.

Christmas stockings are a morning favorite. There are children's gifts ranging from a new toy to a new puppy to liven up Christmas morning. And all children want to see if Santa ate the cookies and drank the milk left out the night before.

Then it's time for Christmas breakfast or brunch together. Often a favorite breakfast or coffeecake makes the day something to look forward to all year. Nana's Star Coffeecake is a favorite at our house or sweet Norwegian thin pancakes called "Tynepanakage" melt in your mouth.

Christmas Day Activities

Gift giving and eating make Christmas Day a time to relax and enjoy each other. Not too much activity is needed beyond that. But you can enhance the fun by putting out family photo albums, playing family movies, showing a Christmas DVD, or playing games.

Singing Christmas carols tells the Christmas story in song; kids playing a musical number on their instrument is fun, as well as talking and sharing around the table.

Take pictures of the family opening gifts, eating together, and enjoying other activities on Christmas Day. It will be special to look back and see the arrangement of people that gathered that year. Every year may seem to be the same, but family members pass on, people move, and Christmas photos can reflect the memories of the changing family and traditions from year to year.

Christmas Dinner Celebrations

Celebrating with relatives and friends who are nearby can occur around noon or late-afternoon for Christmas dinner. A traditional turkey and trimmings meal followed by a gift exchange can be the focus. Scrumptious Christmas desserts are in order, whether a spread of Christmas cookies or pie à la mode.

Being together and sharing food and gifts creates the feeling of belonging and wonderful memory making. One of my favorite holiday traditions happens between Christmas dinner and dessert. In our family, we lower the lights and take turns lighting an individual candle and sharing two blessings from the past year. This draws out the heart of the person in the warm glow of candlelight before dessert is served. When all the candles are lit, we sing "Joy to the World." You can use kernels of Indian corn at Thanksgiving to also share your thankfulness.

Reaching Out

Christmas can also be a painful time for a family rift by divorce, disagreements, and loneliness. Look for people who have no place to go, and invite them over for dinner or dessert. Include them in your joy and help lift their spirits. Check to be sure that coworkers and friends all have someone to be with and places to go. You will be glad to know you tried to include someone rather than finding out afterwards he or she spent Christmas Day alone. This person can add a new dimension to your conversations, games, and fun.

5-Day Countdown till Christmas

Perhaps you're reading this book during the holiday season and you're feeling overwhelmed because Christmas is just a week away. If that's the case, here's what you can do with the time you have left:

Five Days Before:

- Make out a remaining gift list and shop.
- Confirm any invitations and acceptances for Christmas dinner.

Four Days Before:

- Decorate and clean up the house.
- Make a list of menus and grocery list.

Three Days Before:

- Shop for groceries.
- Get laundry out of the way.

Two Days Before:

- Vacuum and clean up any clutter.

One Day Before:

- Set the table.
- Run final errands.

Christmas Eve and Christmas Day:

- Enjoy the days and decide this will be the best Christmas ever.
- Keep ahead of the dishes and meals to keep things organized and peaceful.
- Set aside time to focus on the real meaning of Christmas.

Every holiday turns out different in some way—someone moves, someone marries, little children grow up, and older relatives have fewer years ahead of them than behind them. Whatever the situation, I'm confident you can simplify your plans and handle whatever comes.

Snap a picture of your family and friends enjoying their holiday meal. This pleasant memory will remind you how you decorated your table and what you served that evening.

Refer to any photos you have of Christmas last year and get inspired with how nice they looked. No pictures? No problem. Just get a holiday magazine and be inspired.

> *"The most important entertaining you will do this year, and especially during the Christmas season, will be in your own home with family."*
> *— Emilie Barnes, Christmas is Coming*

Favorite Holiday Traditions

A Christmas tradition is something carried out year after year at the holidays that brings good memories. To find out what are the best traditions in your family you only need to ask these two questions of those you will celebrate with:

1. What do you always do at Christmas?
2. What do you especially enjoy at Christmas?

Here are some examples from people I polled:

Before Christmas:

- "We drive around to see all the Christmas lights and get hot chocolate." A Dad

- "We make handmade ornaments, usually glass with glitter." Junior High Girl

- "We bake cookies and dance to Christmas songs." Grade Schooler

Christmas Eve:

- "We open two gifts on Christmas Eve: a new pair of pajamas for Christmas morning and an ornament for the tree." A Family

- "We have rice pudding with an almond hidden in one person's bowl. The one who has the almond wins a gift prize. We always try to fool others that we have the nut or that we don't have it when we do." A Young Adult

- "We always go to church on Christmas Eve and then come home for my husband's Clam Chowder Soup and Chili." A Wife and Mom

- "We're all together as extended family, talking and catching up with a light supper. The kids put on a Christmas play." A Single Aunt

Christmas Day:

- "We open stockings, eat breakfast, get ready for presents, and have turkey dinner."

- "We like to be home Christmas Day morning for a low-key morning together. Then with family later in the day." Newlywed Couple

- "My father reads a special blessing prayer for the family he wrote years ago even though we are Jewish."

Just ask your family and others what they do at Christmas. It is a rich time of traditions.

How Do You Spend Christmas Day?

Every Christmas is unique in who comes and what happens. Journal what happens and you will have a lovely record and set of memories to look back on over the years. Use a page like this to keep a one page summary.

The people I celebrated with included _____

_____

_____

We gathered together at _____

_____

_____

Things we did on Christmas Eve _____

_____

_____

Our favorite family traditions include _____

_____

_____

My favorite memories of Christmas Day include _____

_____

_____

Next Christmas I want to remember _____

_____

_____

Final Comments _____

_____

_____

Our Favorite Christmas Morning Brunch

Create your own favorite Christmas Morning Breakfast or Brunch menu.

MENU	SERVING PIECE	GROCERY LIST
Day Before:	**The Day:**	**Helpers on The Day:**
Notes:		

Simplifying Your Menu Planning on Christmas Day

The easiest way to simplify holiday meals is to write down what was well-received in the past. The important thing is to be organized and give yourself every chance to succeed in the kitchen.

An Easy Lunch or Light Supper

Create your own favorite Christmas Morning Breakfast or Brunch menu.

MENU	SERVING PIECE	GROCERY LIST
Day Before:	The Day:	Helpers on The Day:
Notes:		

Simplifying Your Menu Planning on Christmas Day
Jot down how long it takes to make your favorite batch of cookies in your recipe so you know from prior years how to get everything ready. Record menus that were big hits with the family, including how long it takes to make. Always organize, then simplify the process.

Christmas Week:
Celebrate Christmas and Enjoy!

Christmas Week _____

Sat.	Sun.	Mon.	Tues.	Wed.	Thurs.	Fri.	Sat.	Sun.

Christmas Eve / Christmas Day

Christmas Eve	Christmas Day

10 Tips to Celebrate Christmas
BY SHARON JAYNES, SPEAKER, AUTHOR AND AVID BLOGGER

While advertisers boast slogans of "new and improved," it is comforting to know that some things never change. Christmas traditions bring comfort and welcome continuity in the safe harbor called home. Make some yearly traditions that matter. It's never too late to start!

1   **Prepare Breakfast the Day Before.** Plan ahead with a breakfast recipe you can prepare the night before and pop in the oven on Christmas morning. Keep the cook happy, too.

2   **Open Your Home to Others.** Christmas can be a joyful time of the year surrounded by family and friends exchanging gifts and hugs. But for many, Christmas is a depressing time that echoes feelings of loneliness and isolation. Ask someone to join you.

3   **Expand Your Circle.** Invite a college student away from home, a widow, divorcee or single friend, or a homeless man or woman to share your celebration. Give them a gift. Let them help you with the cleanup. That will really make them feel at home!

4   **Make Coupon Booklets for Your Children.** A coupon could be for one game of Monopoly, an hour past curfew, a restaurant dinner, or a week of double allowance.

5   **Make a Coupon Booklet for Your Spouse.** Come up with your own suggestions and they probably won't cost any money! Take over a task, or plan a weekend away.

6   **Give a Treasure.** Give a relative or a friend something of yours that they always admired. This will convince them of your love for them and reflect real generosity.

7   **Give Each Child a Christmas Ornament that Reflects Their Interests.** When they marry, give them the collection as a wedding gift. (Buy yourself an extra box of tissues.)

8   **Create a Christmas Eve Tradition.** On Christmas Eve read the original Christmas story of the Nativity story by candlelight before going to bed. Remember why we celebrate.

9   **Light a Candle to Remind You of the Significance of Christmas Day.** Keep a special white candle lit the entire Christmas Day to remind everyone of the very first Christmas.

10   **Capture the Memories in a Christmas Photo Album.** Take photos of everyone at your Christmas Day celebration and place them in a separate Christmas album. Write down who was there and any special memories you created together.

Sharon Jaynes is an international speaker, avid blogger and author of 17 books including The Power of a Woman's Words, I'm Not Good Enough and Other Lies Women Tell Themselves, *and* Becoming the Woman of His Dreams. *Her books have sold over a half million copies. She lives in N.C. with her husband, Steve. Visit* **sharonjaynes.com**

Christmas is Here!

1. Simplify your Christmas Celebrations by asking your family or people you celebrate with what they like to do. Honor their requests and build good memories together.
2. Plan your holiday meals ahead with favorite traditional foods and menus that you like to make.
3. Focus on the spiritual side of Christmas with readings or celebrating with those of your faith.

Personal Reflection

1. One of my favorite times of Christmas celebrations is _____

   _____

2. My Christmas Eve and Christmas Day celebrations are good when _____

   _____

3. We celebrate Christmas by _____

   _____

Holiday Support Group Discussion Questions

1. What are you looking forward to this Christmas?
2. What will make it a special time?
3. Who will you be celebrating with?
4. What is a favorite memory of your Christmas childhood?
5. What will it be like where you are on Christmas Day?
6. If you could change one thing about Christmas, what would it be?
7. Something new I'd like to try _____

   _____

> *For the original Christmas story, you can read it in my companion booklet, Simply December Devotions or in Luke chapter 2. The nativity story includes questions to engage children and adults as well as December 1-25 Days of inspirational devotionals. Be sure to include the spiritual component in your celebration time.*

11

New Year's and the End of the Year

One Week to Go and Celebrate the New Year

If the holiday season is a marathon, then New Year's and the week after Christmas is the last lap. You can take it at any speed you want. Just be sure to finish well with a plan in mind.

Did you have a good Christmas? I hope so because you still have one more week to enjoy before the year ends and the new year begins. New Year's week, New Year's Eve, and New Year's Day are your opportunities to plug in more living any way you'd like.

The week between Christmas and New Year's is like an entire "Bonus Week" since kids are still out of school, work has slowed down or you have vacation time away from work. What can you do with those days? Here are some things you may not have thought about.

The Day After Christmas

It's a good time to relax, still converse with family guests, and continue the Christmas holiday together. You can start to get your home cleaned up from the gift wrappings and put the kitchen back in shape from the festive foods you prepared. It's time to slow down your internal drive and take a day off.

For others it's out the door to the "Day after Christmas Sales." Wal-Mart reports the Day after Christmas is the biggest day of gift card redemption. It's also the day to find online discounts to purchase gift cards at a discount, which may be perfect for birthdays in the upcoming year. Or you could extend your holiday generosity to purchase them for needy folks you've met.

Heading to the mail for returns and bargains with family or a friend might be the excitement you need. And Christmas decorations are on sale. Just remember that whatever you buy, you need to store them for the next year.

Ask your friends what they are doing the week between Christmas and New Year's and you might find their suggestions help you clarify your personal choice for this year. Will you relax, cleanup and catch-up, or get away for a few days?

The Week Between Christmas and New Year's

There are lots of ways to spend the week while some are better than others for you. Look at your calendars from the past couple years and see what you actually did this week. Those activities will probably work well again. Or you may find you prefer something different. Whatever helps you wrap up the old year and get ready for the new is a good choice.

For personal time you might sleep in, go to a movie, have extended family over or finish a project you've been wanting to do. Nothing launches the new year better than completing a task such as clearing away paper piles, a decorating spruce up, or visiting your financial planner for year-end decisions. Do something new like spending a day skiing, sightseeing locally, or planning a family outing for a day. Make your week memorable and even productive.

End of the Year Sales

Take advantage of end of the year sales for new clothes or just to see all the bargains. You could put together a whole new wardrobe on a limited budget with the extra time to shop and search for the best of the best. Retailers want to end the year in the black so markdowns are their ticket to get you back in the door. Go through your closet and see what you could use to complete an outfit or two.

Technology is going to be on sale, too, to clear out year-end merchandise. You may be able to exceed preholiday sales with 40%-70% off providing what you want is still available. Make any returns you need to and check online for even more deals.

Your budget is definitely something to consider so plan it out or use cash so you don't put yourself in the "hole" getting good deals.

New Year's Eve

Do you like to party on New Year's Eve? Or stay up and watch the Times Square Ball Drop on TV? This is your night to celebrate. Be sure to see our tips in this chapter for throwing a New Year's Eve party.

My son-in-law remembers his grandmother cutting up confetti to throw at midnight. Today you can go through old files (which you probably need to anyway) and send them through your shredding machine. Voila! You have New Year's Eve confetti for midnight and a clean file drawer.

If you are more reflective consider listing all the good things that happened in the past year. Mark Victor Hansen, coauthor of *Chicken Soup for the Soul*, recommends doing so before you write your New Year's resolutions. Gratefulness is a springboard for making good resolutions for the year ahead.

New Year's Day

New Year's Day can include the tradition of watching the Rose Bowl Parade on TV in the morning and the Fiesta Bowl Football game in the afternoon. It's also a good day to take down decorations, write thank-you notes, and start the new year fresh. Put up your brand new calendars for the year ahead and anticipate all the wonderful people and things that will come into your life.

New Year's Resolutions, Goals, and Bucket List

January 1 is the day to write a resolution or two. If you're not living the life you love or at least enjoying each day, then perhaps it's because you don't know what you want, you know what it is but haven't worked to get it, or you've let life get in your way. Here are three ways to change that while you are poised at the beginning of the new year.

Pick One Style for a New Year, New You

A New Year's Resolution is a January 1 personal commitment for the coming year to change a habit or lifestyle for the better such as the two most popular ones, to lose weight and get organized!

A Goal is a dream with a plan attached and is best achieved if there is a positive emotional response to its success, such as moving to a warm climate, redecorating at home, or doubling your income. Jot them on your new monthly calendar.

A Bucket List is a wish list of things you'd like to do in your lifetime that captures your imagination such as climbing Mt. Everest, running a marathon, or writing a book. Fill your bucket list with 5-10 things you've only dreamed about.

What Would it Take for a "New Year, New You" Lifestyle Makeover?

Here is a list of 15 ideas to stimulate your thinking. Write your own list of eight to ten goals you would like to have or do in the coming new year. Think big!

- Prioritize my life and say "no" with confidence.
- Find a regular exercise program I like.
- Eat healthier every meal.
- Get to bed by 10:30 p.m.
- Reorganize and upgrade my office.
- Create a budget and save for my dream car.
- Plan one enjoyable activity per 52 weekends.
- Trade childcare for more personal time.
- Get together monthly with a good friend.
- Become team manager for your son's sports team.
- Go on my bucket list dream vacation.
- Call parents/grandparents once a week.
- Send out birthday cards (or birthday emails) on time.
- Join a new business group.
- Wrap up leadership responsibility in current organization.
- Complete a degree over the next three years.

Event-Planning Worksheet

Event _____ Date _____

Party Idea

Theme:

Invitees

-

Save the Date:
Invitations:

Menu

Beverages:

Food:

Decorations

Table:

Other:

Entertainment

Prizes:

When & Where

10 Tips for a New Year's Party
BY BRENDA LAURENCE, WRITER AND SPEAKER

New Year celebrations are a milestone celebration contrasting the past and the future. You can ask guests to dress in black and white and bring an old photo of themselves. Carry the black-and-white color scheme with extra glitter and glamour through the decorations, food, and conversation at your party of "Out with the Old and In with the New."

Your celebration can be a formal party or a simple, casual evening shared with friends. This event comes at the close of a long holiday season of entertaining. It's a perfect time for bring-a-dish dinners, party paper plates and a white elephant gift exchange. Try these party suggestions and group conversation starters for your event:

1. Display the guests' photos. Give a prize to whoever guesses the most correctly.

2. Ask the difference between writing a Bucket List and a New Year's Resolution and which one your guests are most likely to do.

3. What in the old year are you glad to leave behind?

4. What are you hoping to find in the New Year?

5. You've decided to write a bucket-list for the New Year. What's on your list?

6. What is one resolution you plan to keep?

7. What new beginning in your life has been very positive?

8. What wisdom have you gained from last year that you want to remember for the new year?

9. Play an old party game like Charades or Catchphrase and then play a newer game, i.e., Imagine If or Apples to Apples that includes everyone.

10. As midnight approaches, encourage guests to clear their minds of regrets and disappointments by writing a "Regret Card" and a "Bucket List" for the new year on another card. On the "10-Second Countdown" have guests tear up their Regret Card and toss them as confetti into a fireplace leaving the old behind. Celebrate the new year by waving and sharing their Bucket List.

With the conversation and activity suggestions above, your guests will leave the party and old year behind with great expectation of a beautiful future. Every beginning brings new hope, new energy, and new plans.

*Brenda Laurence is a speaker and author of numerous magazine articles and small group curriculum. She is passionate about strengthening relationships in couples, families and friends through home entertaining and meaningful conversation. Brenda and her husband are founders and authors of Encounter Marriage Weekends. Visit **encountermarriageweekend.com***

"Out with The Old, Make Room for the New"

The Last Week of the Year

The week between Christmas and New Year's may be your long-awaited catch-up week. Here are some organizing tips to intentionally improve your life at home or work. Pick something that would make the most positive difference in your life for the new year. It's the annual time for a fresh start in your life.

Home

Put away any countertop clutter or holiday decorations. When you see flat surfaces cleaned off and you've done a quick vacuuming, your home will look much cleaner. This is also a good time to go through a clothes closet a day with each child or family member and donate to charities that need extra clothing in the winter months.

Paperwork

Go through paper piles and get paper projects listed on a Master List, file papers that need to be put away, and clean up your desktop. Nothing starts the new year better than a clear desk and work surface.

Email

This is the perfect time to clean out your email inbox by reading and deleting, or categorically deleting anything over six months old. Create and move emails into files marked by three-month time frames and the year. That way they are still accessible with the "Search" feature, but you have a clean inbox.

Finances

This is the time to balance your checkbook and list a summary of your savings and expenses for the year. Organize your financial papers in files by credit cards, receipts, utilities, major purchases and home repairs. Tax preparation will be so much easier once you've done this.

Work

As a Professional Organizer and Business Coach I've often organized client offices during the week between Christmas and New Year's since so few people are in the office. The client is able to focus on organizing and is visibly more productive when the year begins. It's worth heading into work for one day to get the office cleaned up.

File Drawers

This is a good time to clean out file drawers by starting in the back and working to the front. Shred and toss what you no longer need. Now everything is mostly digital so it's good to either scan papers or eliminate them completely. Keep your paper drawers current.

Be sure to pick only one of the previous projects—the one that would give you the most satisfaction when completed. You're about to begin a new year! Let go of the old and get ready for the new by organizing your surroundings. Begin with controlling your space and belongings and you'll find the next year more efficient and effective.

10 Tips for Holiday Vacation Time with Kids

BY CARLA YOUNG, PUBLISHER OF MOMEOMAGAZINE.COM

1 **Start the Holiday Organized.** Don't wait until the kids are out of school before doing all your planning and organizing. Complete whatever you can beforehand so you can start the holiday break feeling relaxed and prepared for what's ahead.

2 **Declutter Your Schedule.** It's tempting to overbook ourselves when the invitations start rolling in. Resist. Pick and choose which holiday parties you would love to attend and be realistic about the ones you have no choice about, and tactfully decline the others.

3 **Find a Friend.** Switching from school life to family time can be a little challenging for social kids. Find out which of their friends are staying in town for the holidays and plan a few special activities that include their friends.

4 **Redirect the Energy.** Take that holiday excitement and redirect it into a physical activity. It's tempting to stay indoors, especially if the weather isn't cooperating, but be sure to plan activities that get everyone outside and burning up extra energy!

5 **Stock Up on Craft Supplies.** Check the craft supply closet to make sure you have all the necessary ingredients for a creative afternoon making items with a holiday theme. Enlist the kids' help making holiday decorations.

6 **Bake a Lifetime of Memories.** There's something about an afternoon spent baking as a family. Even the smallest members of the family can help put sprinkles on cookies or mix up the cookie dough.

7 **Plan Both A and B.** Expect the unexpected and always have a plan A and a plan B. The holidays are about spending time with your family so be flexible.

8 **Ask Them to Self-Entertain.** Give kids plenty of options to amuse themselves. Set up play stations in their bedrooms and play rooms to allow kids to 'self-serve' their fun.

9 **Plan a Few Surprises.** Buy a new craft, game or movie to pull out "in case of emergency" when spirits are low and boredom has set in. The novelty alone will buy you an afternoon of peace and quiet.

10 **Give Yourself the Gift of Downtime.** Don't forget about yourself in all your holiday planning. Ask your significant other (or even better, the grandparents) to take the kids to give you a break. You aren't allowed to use the break to run holiday errands — it's all about you!

Carla Young is the proud mother of one very precocious daughter, a loving wife to one lucky husband, and a supporter of moms who want to build a business that gives them the flexibility to work-from-home and raise a family. She shares her time management, motivation and business tips for mom entrepreneurs at **momeomagazine.com**

New Year's and Year End

HAPPY NEW YEAR

1. The week between Christmas and New Year's is like a "bonus" week to do things out of the ordinary routine — spend time with family, shop or clean out and catch up. Use it intentionally.
2. New Year's Eve and New Year's Day are excellent times to close down the past year and plan a gathering with friends.
3. Spend the extra time with your kids and grandkids to create memories while they are home.

Personal Reflection

1. One of my favorite ways to celebrate the New Year is _____

    _____

2. New Year's Eve and New Year's Day are times when I like to _____

    _____

3. We spend the week between Christmas and New Year's _____

    _____

Holiday Support Group Discussion Questions

1. What will you be doing the week between Christmas and New Year's this year?

2. Are you a bargain shopper and where do you like to go?

3. What were the biggest one or two highlights of last year?

4. What are you looking forward to in the new year?

5. Do you make New Year's resolutions?

6. Have you ever had a New Year's Eve party?

7. Something new I'd like to try _____

    _____

> *I love fresh new calendars. They are a place to dream of "Things to Do, Places to Go, and People to See" just like our Holiday Season theme. The good news is the future will likely be better than the past because of all your rich life experiences and the person you've become. Look forward to it and have faith the best is yet to come!*

12

Wrap Up the Holiday Season Successfully

Start the New Year Fresh

*Wrap up your memories, the holiday decorations, and your final lists
on what made this year a wonderful holiday season — Thanksgiving, Christmas and New Year's.
The secret to simplifying every season hereafter is keeping notes and continue doing what you do well.*

You're finished! Well almost. The final tasks include putting away the decorations, and reflecting on your holiday memories. How do you do that? By completing a final checklist and putting your home back in shape. It's not that hard and hopefully you can complete it in an afternoon or a weekend.

Checklist for Wrapping Up the Holiday Season

- ☑ Put Decorations Away
- ☑ Make One Clean, Final Master Gift List to Save
- ☑ Write Thank You Notes
- ☑ Fill Out the One Page "My Journal of Holiday Reflections"
- ☑ Place Your Holiday Photos in a Holiday Photo Book or Label Digitally
- ☑ Return Any Gifts
- ☑ Finish Up Any Details

There you've finished! Congratulations on turning the most stressful time of year into a memorable one for family and friends. Be sure to write down the compliments from family and friends on how well you did.

My personal highlights came when one of my daughters said, "Mom, this was such a peaceful holiday." All because I wrote and followed the eight-week Holiday Calendar Plan.

Better yet, my son-in-law said, "This was the BEST Christmas I've ever had!" That was worth every moment. When asked why, he thoughtfully said, "No drama." Chaos and stress are "out" and peace and joy are "in" when you simplify the whole season. You can do it, too!

My Journal of Holiday Reflections

THE BEST THINGS THAT HAPPENED THIS CHRISTMAS _____YEAR_____

This year I so enjoyed _____

_____

My thoughts on how things went in each of the following areas:

Gifts _____

_____

_____

Cards _____

_____

_____

Decorations _____

_____

_____

Activities _____

_____

_____

The Best Event(s) _____

_____

_____

The Best Memory of the Season _____

_____

_____

Next Year I Want to Be Sure to _____

_____

_____

Final Thoughts: _____

_____

_____

Congratulations on bringing joy to others at this holiday season. See you next year!

Simplify the Holiday Season Testimonials

Don't take my word for it that you can simplify your holidays. Look at these audience remarks! Everyone took charge of simplifying at least one area. What will yours be?

"The first thing I'm going to simplify for my holidays is get a calendar and write events AND plan gift gifting." — Miriam W.

"I decided to "enjoy" the holidays instead of just surviving." —Linda S.

~~~~~~~~~~~

"The first thing I'm going to simplify for my holidays is organize my gift wrap items." — Diane M.

"The first thing I'm going to simplify for my holidays is keep my budget with less gifts." — Sammye H.

"I especially appreciated the Master Gift List! " —Lisa C.

" I like the idea of 3 gifts per child." —Chequita F.

~~~~~~~~~~~

"I learned to keep my Christmas cards simple and start early." — Gail H.

"The first thing I'm going to simplify for my holidays is to remember to buy one design of Christmas card each year." —Berni M.

"The first thing I'm going to simplify for my holidays is start cards early and write a letter." — Carmen D.

~~~~~~~~~~~

"The first thing I'm going to simplify for my holidays is culling out decorations and donating them." — Betsy M.

"I will start decorating earlier so we can enjoy more." — Jane G.

"The first thing I'm going to simplify for my holidays is sort the decorations and give some away." — Jean J.

~~~~~~~~~~~

"When I go home the first thing I am going to organize is my cookie list." — Jeanne L.

"The first thing I'm going to simplify for my holidays is gather recipes!" — Gail D.

"The first thing I'm going to simplify for my holidays is participate in the cookie exchange and freeze." — Debbie R.

~~~~~~~~~~~

" I especially appreciated the idea to combine visits with family and friends with events." —Pam F.

"Take lots of pictures and enjoy special moments with family and friends!" — Terri L.

~~~~~~~~~~~

"I decided to use your calendar idea." — Nancy M.

"I learned that the three weeks before Christmas are too busy. Start now!" — Colleen P.

"I appreciated your helpfulness in getting more organized and simplifying things in order to enjoy the holidays." — Patricia V.

"The first thing I'm going to simplify for my holidays is to have a willing, positive, and helpful heart." — Terri L.

You can watch the "Simplify Your Holidays" speech these women heard live on DVD available at **organizingpro.com/store**. Be inspired to simplify your life!

How Did YOU Like the Holidays?

It's always good to journal your own thoughts. Here are some to get you started. The holidays are good if you are happy. YOU are the key to a good season.

1. What did you like most about the holiday season? Check off or rate on a scale of 1-10.

    _____ Exchanging gifts with family and friends

    _____ Decorating the house inside and out

    _____ Sending Christmas cards and a family letter

    _____ Contributing time or money to charities

    _____ Attending special holiday events

    _____ Baking cookies and specialty food

    _____ Enjoying the extra time with family at home

    _____ Spending the vacation doing something memorable

2. If I could only do one thing better this Christmas, I would really like to _____

    _____

    _____

3. If I could change one thing about the holidays, I would _____

    _____

    _____

4. One way I enjoyed reaching out to others this season was _____

    _____

    _____

5. The two most memorable moments were _____

    _____

    _____

6. The things I really enjoyed about this holiday season were _____

    _____

    _____

My Notes for Next Year

Highlights to Do Again

_____

_____

_____

_____

_____

_____

People We Celebrated With

_____

_____

_____

_____

_____

_____

Best Places to Shop

_____

_____

_____

_____

_____

_____

Ways I Simplified This Year

_____

_____

_____

_____

_____

_____

Personal Perks of the Season

_____

_____

_____

_____

_____

_____

Remember for Next Year!

_____

_____

_____

_____

_____

_____

My Actual Holiday Season

It's always good to jot down what actually happened as a reference point. It sets you up for success next year.

Calendar Tips
for the Holiday Season

	Monday	Tuesday	Wednesday	Thursday	Friday	Saturday	Sunday
8 Weeks ❑ Fill in Gift List ❑ Mark Calendar ❑ Wrapping Center							
7 Weeks ❑ Buy 1/3 Gifts ❑ Cards & Stamps ❑ Event Page							
6 Weeks ❑ Buy 2/3 gifts ❑ Wrap Gifts ❑ Write Cards							
5 Weeks ❑ Thanksgiving ❑ Plan Menus ❑ Use Friday Well							
4 Weeks ❑ Finish Gifts ❑ Finish Wrapping ❑ Start Decorations							
3 Weeks ❑ Decorate Home ❑ Address Cards ❑ Host Event							
2 Weeks ❑ Bake Cookies ❑ Clean Home ❑ Donations							
1 Week ❑ Enjoy Events ❑ Finish Bake ❑ Social Media							
Christmas ❑ Celebrate! ❑ Exchange Gifts ❑ Attend Services							
New Year ❑ Celebrate! ❑ Put Away Decorations							

Side labels: Plan, Shop, Wrap | Mail & Decor | Celebrations

10 Time Tips for the Holidays

BY MARCIA RAMSLAND, THE ORGANIZINE PRO

Brighten up your calendar—and your outlook—with holiday stickers or a red pen marking holiday events.

1. Buy gifts in one major category this year—different sweaters for everyone, appropriate CDs or books for mailed gifts, or personalized restaurant gift certificates.

2. Mark your calendar with two-hour appointments for Christmas preparations such as Thursday bake, Friday decorate, Saturday shop and clean.

3. Enlist a holiday buddy to help you plan, especially one who is better in an area where you are weak.

4. When you're doing the family Christmas card, get an assembly line going. After you have addressed the envelopes, line them up to stuff and stamp. Kids will love to participate.

5. Shop for convenience, whether it be online or at one mall to simplify the abundance of choices.

6. Call or e-mail the person for whom you can't find that special gift. Ask her what she would really like to get this year.

7. Stretch your limited social time by attending a Christmas event and getting together with friends for dinner beforehand or dessert afterwards.

8. Purchase a holiday book like *Simply December Devotions* or novel to curl up with each night to get you through the season.

9. Brighten up your calendar—and your outlook—with holiday stickers or a red pen marking holiday events.

10. Savor one event or daily conversation by jotting it down in a Christmas journal. Title it "The Best Things that Happened to Me This Christmas."

(Excerpt from *Simply Your Life; Get Organized and Stay that Way!* by Marcia Ramsland, Thomas Nelson Publishing.)

Marcia Ramsland is well known as "The Organizing Pro" for her practical skills and tips to manage busy lives. She is the author of the first book in the Women of Faith Lifestyles line, Simplify Your Life: Get Organized and Stay that Way! *She offers organizing resources and free tips at her website* **organizingpro.com**

Wrap Up the Holiday Season Successfully

1. To finish the season successfully complete the final activities: decorations away, a final Master Gift List, Thank You notes, and holiday photos organized.
2. Spice up your memories by printing your holiday photos for a Holiday Photo Book. Or label your digital photos so you can easily find them next year.
3. Journal how the season went and keep notes for yourself.

Personal Reflection

1. Some of my favorite memories of the season were _____

   _____

2. Personally I amazed myself this season by _____

   _____

3. This year was different because _____

   _____

Holiday Support Group Discussion Questions

1. What was your favorite part of Thanksgiving, Christmas or New Year's this year?

2. What was especially touching?

3. What was particularly stressful and could it have been avoided?

4. What did you do to organize and simplify your decorations as you put them away?

5. Will you be keeping holiday photos of this year?

6. Have you finished the season with a final Master Gift List and Holiday Season Calendar of what you actually did?

7. Something new I'd like to try _____

   _____

> *Rediscover the joy of the season. Happy Thanksgiving, Merry Christmas, and Happy New Year to you and yours—one holiday at a time!*

Appendix

Lifestyle Experts
"10 Best Tips for the Holidays"

A Final Word from the Author

*T*hank you for reading *Simplify Your Holiday Season* and sharing your time with me. It was a joy to write and create new ways to simplify the season for you! I've always been passionate about taking complicated things in life and making them easier for people to do through speaking and writing. And the holidays can be complicated!

Since I feel simplifying the holiday season is such an important topic, this is actually the third holiday book I've written and designed myself. My first book was "My Holiday Notebook" which I almost quit doing after several years until Better Homes and Gardens featured the tips from it in 2006. To create the holiday notebook, I'd purchase white 3 ring notebooks and dividers at the office store and invite friends and family to assemble each one around my dining room table. I did this for several years and it helped hundreds of people.

My second book, *Simplify Your Holidays*, was a beautiful 3-ring professionally printed planner by Thomas Nelson in 2008. But alas, problems with the binder rings caused it to go out of print. I was quite sad that it was no longer available in the marketplace.

Thankfully my Agent and my publisher arranged for me to print my own version, which you are holding in your hands or reading as an ebook. It contains 60% new material including everything in chapters 7-12 plus other information and charts in earlier chapters. I'm delighted that this is the perfect time in digital history to keep you updated annually with downloadable Holiday Season Calendar charts! Now everyone can have a peaceful holiday season.

A Personal Note

Personally over the years I've taken the chaos out of the holiday season by setting up a new system each year starting with Gift Giving. By trimming down the long list and expectations of mailing to relatives in five states and instead giving to just those in our immediate family, I breathed a huge sigh of relief. And we are still close to extended family which I love.

Also moving from a live tree to a 3-piece pre-lit tree over the years has lowered our marital stress. Thank you, David!

And making the shift from mailing all postage based Christmas cards to over half email greetings, has freed up my time and budget to help others simplify their holidays by speaking and teaching online holiday classes. We are all happier that way.

Appreciation Makes the Effort Worthwhile

For those of us that live a packed full life the rest of the year, the holidays can add pressure that can keep us stressed and up at night covering all the bases. However I absolutely love our family together time when our kids and spouses come for several days. Finally I feel like I can handle it with ease — just in time to welcome new toddler grandchildren and a puppy to the mix of all of us at our house. I still keep that busy schedule until they come, but I've learned to simplify all the things I've written about and you can, too!

The most meaningful compliments come from family. My one daughter looked around the house at the end of Christmas week one year and said thoughtfully, "This was a... "peaceful" week being here. Thank you."

One of my son-in-laws said, "This was the best Christmas ever!" When pressed as to why, he replied after some time and said, "No drama." It was worth pursuing systems to make holidays peaceful for myself and our family guests. Everyone needs a welcoming place to relax over the holidays.

Readers' Holiday Stories

I would be delighted to hear your personal holiday story of how things have improved for you, too. Just email me your story through my website www.organizingpro.com. Here are two emails that came within days after the holidays last year that might inspire you further.

Dear Marcia,

Now that the holidays are over, I can doubly say that I am sure I would have missed something without all the pre-planning that "Simplify the Holidays" helps with. This is my second year to use it and I kept notes from last year, so I didn't have to rethink things like Christmas menus and my list of baked goods.

I start in October by reading the book through and making a few notes and copying planning pages. Then in November I start the 8 week plan and it keeps me on track. I constantly check my gift lists to see what I have and need to buy. In December I enjoyed reading your December daily devotions. They keep my mind calm and I felt less stress over gifts and baking, and I enjoyed the time with my family.

As a side note: This year my five children, two spouses, and four grandchildren were together for the first time in three years! We gathered at my daughter's spacious home and had a wonderful reunion and time of fellowship. Have a Happy New Year!

—Gale Walker
Foresthill, CA

Dear Marcia.

I just wanted to tell you how much your "Simplify Your Holidays" book has blessed me. I started using it three years ago, and it has made such a difference. My Christmas plans are not nearly as hectic as they used to be.

This year was the biggest test of all: I followed your plan, did all of my shopping early, but then I got terribly sick on December 23. Although I can't say I enjoyed the holiday, my family was still able to move forward with celebrations.

All the gifts were bought and wrapped in advance and all the food had been purchased. My husband was able to put everything in boxes and change the venue since I was unable to host. If I hadn't followed your plan, I'm not sure what would have happened.

Thanks for your great ideas and strategies. You helped save the day!

—Tammy Stevenson
St. Louis, MO

How can you simplify your holidays? Keep what is working and just change what is not until it works smoothly. I have every confidence in you that this year will be different!

I often ask my audiences when I speak, "Can you do that?" Now you can respond with a resounding, "I can do that — and will!" Happy Thanksgiving, Merry Christmas, and Happy New Years!

Sincerely,
Marcia Ramsland
—The Organizing Pro and Holiday Coach

About the Author

*M*arcia Ramsland is a media personality, speaker, author, and professional organizer whose passion is to teach people practical ways to live life well with focus and accomplishment. She helps clients and audience participants conquer organization problems to simplify their lives and lifestyles. She is the president of The Organizing Pro & Co. She and her husband live in San Diego, and are the parents of three young adult married children. She speaks nationally and appears on radio and TV, including Martha Stewart Radio, and in national magazines like Better Homes and Gardens and Real Simple magazines. Her earlier holiday book was featured in Better Homes and Gardens Special Organizing edition and she was Spokesperson for Sam's Club for Holiday Entertaining.

To contact Marcia for speaking engagements or for sharing how this book has changed your life, email or contact:

Marcia Ramsland, The Organizing Pro

E-mail: **Marcia@organizingpro.com** * (858) 217-6320
www.organizingpro.com

Books by Marcia Ramsland:

- *Simplify Your Life: Get Organized and Stay That Way!*

- *Simplify Your Time: Stop Running and Start Living!*

- *Simplify Your Space: Create Order and Reduce Stress!*

- *Ages and Stages of Getting Children Organized (Booklet)*

- *Simplify Your Holiday Season: Turn Seasonal Stress into Holiday Success!*

- *Simply December Devotions: 25 Days to Celebrate the Real Meaning of Christmas*

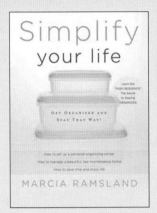  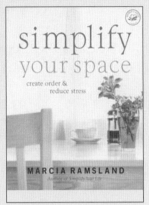

Book Dedication

❄

This book is dedicated to my amazing husband, David, our wonderful three children Christy, Lisa and Mark and their delightful spouses. A special dedication goes to our growing number of the most beautiful grandchildren in the world. I love each of you!

As a family we have been fortunate to spend the holidays together in some fashion and I am so blessed because of everyone's effort to do so. Christmas wouldn't be Christmas without you and the Reason for the Season.

Also, this book is dedicated to YOU, the Reader. May you find peace and joy as you simplify the season each year.

I believe you can face whatever comes your way with grace. As we say in all my speeches, You can do it, Girlfriend! May God bless you as you celebrate the holiday season.

My Notes

Simplify to Succeed!

❄

Remember the holidays are as much a matter of organization as they are a matter of the heart.

Get better at both each year to fully enjoy the holiday season from now on!

Visit www.organizingpro.com Today!